2/04

Democratic Republic of the Congo

Democratic Republic of the Congo

BY TERRI WILLIS

Enchantment of the World
Second Series

Children's Press®

A Division of Scholastic Inc.

New York   Toronto   London   Auckland   Sydney
Mexico City   New Delhi   Hong Kong
Danbury, Connecticut

Frontispiece: Children of Congo on a village path

Consultant: Edouard Bustin, Professor of Political Science, African Studies Center,
            Boston University, Boston, MA

Please note: All statistics are as up-to-date as possible at the time of publication.

Book production by Herman Adler Design

Library of Congress Cataloging-in-Publication Data

Willis, Terri.
  Democratic Republic of the Congo / by Terri Willis.
          p. cm. — (Enchantment of the world. Second series)
Includes bibliographical references and index.
  ISBN 0-516-24250-4
  1. Congo (Democratic Republic)—Juvenile literature. [1. Congo (Democratic Republic)]
I. Title. II. Series.
  DT652.W542003
  967.51—dc21   2003000504

Democratic Republic of the Congo

Cover photo:
Congolese on the
Mongala River

Contents

Congolese children

Luba mask

Collapsing Under Its Wealth

THE DEMOCRATIC REPUBLIC OF THE CONGO—CONGO, AS it is commonly known—holds some of the greatest natural wealth in the continent of Africa. At the start of the twentieth century Congo provided elephant tusks for ivory and rubber to make tires for a new invention, the automobile. Later the sale of mined diamonds earned millions of dollars for the country. Today mines in Congo provide coltan (columbite-tantalite), an important metallic ore used in the manufacture of cell phones, computers, and home video games. The country's soil is fertile and capable of growing crops. There are waterways that supply a bounty of fish. Vast forests keep many logging firms in business.

Even though the country is rich in natural resources, it is collapsing. Many of its people are dying from starvation, disease, and war. Children's bellies are bloated from severe malnutrition. Yet they are lucky to be alive. In parts of Congo, three out of every four babies born die before they reach the age of two. There are few jobs, schools, or hospitals in Congo. Water sources are polluted, and roads, what few there are, are mostly dirt paths, grooved and full of potholes.

Opposite: **Diamonds are one of the Democratic Republic of the Congo's greatest natural resources.**

This main road delays travelers due to its poor condition.

Congolese flee their homes after an attack by Rwandan militia.

Why does a country with so much natural wealth suffer from such hardships? The blame lies precisely with the natural wealth itself. It is a magnet to those who wish to rob the land and the people who live on it.

For more than a century people from outside Congo have entered and taken whatever they could harvest. It began with the slave trade and continued with King Leopold II of Belgium (1865–1909). He used Congo as if it were his own treasure chest, taking out valuable ivory and rubber, and making the people of Congo his slaves. The brutality he inflicted upon the people and the land is nearly unequaled in all of history.

Today there are seven or eight armies fighting over the land and its riches. Battles are being fought in Congo and several of its neighboring countries, particularly Rwanda and Uganda. The killers even steal food and money sent to Congo by charitable organizations to feed starving children. Innocent citizens travel from refugee camp to refugee camp, country to country, hoping to avoid the devastation. Eventually, many just flee into the rain forest. There, they try to hide in peace, but there are no services for them: no food, fresh water, or medical care. Diseases such as malaria and cholera take many lives, while more starve to death. Some estimates put the death toll at 2,500 people a day. Many say the situation in the Congo is the worst humanitarian crisis in the world.

Still, the whole of Congo is not starving. While the country is not economically wealthy by any measure, in places many people are managing to put together a decent living. There the people are fortunate enough to have food, and children can attend school. There is time for entertainment and time to enjoy sports. The economy is weak throughout the nation, but some people have jobs and others earn money by

This Congolese tailor is fortunate enough to own his own shop and earn a living for himself.

Homes in rural villages do not have electricity or running water.

working on their own. Some people live in rural areas, getting most of their income from agriculture. Those who live in cities mainly have jobs in manufacturing or service industries.

Congo is a country of great extremes. While many starve, there are a few who are fabulously wealthy, some even living in mansions near the refugee camps. Some cities are growing rapidly, others are disappearing as their citizens flee for their lives or die. People who live in rural areas often live much like people did centuries ago with few modern conveniences such as electricity or piped water. However, people in cities have access to television and computers, fancy restaurants, universities, libraries, museums, and professional sporting events. Underlying all these lifestyles is one simple truth: Congo is a nation with vast and valuable resources. The differences lie in just how those resources are used.

Officially, the country's name is the Democratic Republic of the Congo, as it had been known before 1972. This is the same country that was once known as the Belgian Congo and then, from 1972 until 1997, Zaire. Another country, the Republic of the Congo, lies just to the west. There are several ways to differentiate the two. Sometimes the Democratic

Republic of the Congo is shortened to an abbreviation: DRC. Other times it is known as Congo-Kinshasa, after its capital city, while the Republic of the Congo is known as Congo-Brazzaville, for its capital. But often, in the popular press, the Democratic Republic of the Congo is simply called Congo. That term will be used throughout this book. When the Republic of the Congo is being discussed, its full name will be used.

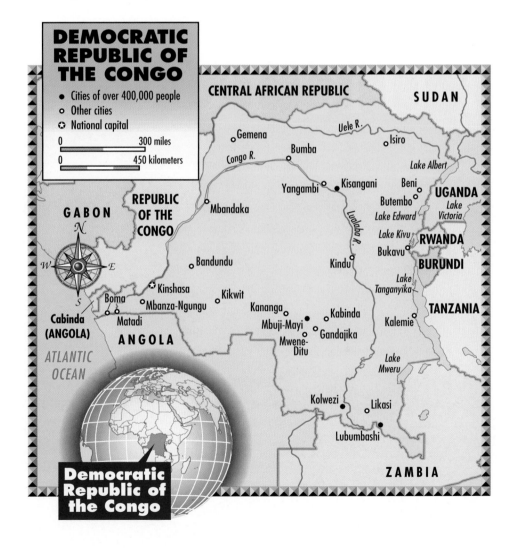

The Country and the River

ONGO IS AFRICA'S THIRD-LARGEST COUNTRY. ONLY Algeria and Sudan are larger. Considered a part of central Africa, it is bordered by the Republic of the Congo, the Central African Republic, Sudan, Uganda, Rwanda, Burundi, Tanzania, Zambia, Angola, and the Atlantic Ocean. The entire length of Lake Tanganyika lies along its eastern border with Burundi and Tanzania. The Congo River forms part of the border with the Congo Republic.

Much of the geography of Congo is influenced by the river that gave it its name, the Congo. The Congo River basin, the area that drains into the river, makes up the core of the country, but there is more. Uplands north and south of the basin, both with similar types of terrain and plant life, are another geographical region, as are the country's eastern highlands. There is also a small coastal region, a 25-mile-wide (40-kilometer) strip where the Congo River meets the Atlantic Ocean.

Opposite: **Hills rise behind the lush savanna on the border of Burundi and the Congo.**

The Congo River Basin is the largest basin in Africa, covering 12 percent of the continent. It is covered by rain forests and surrounded on all sides by hills and mountains.

The Congo River Basin

The Congo River basin is the area in which all the rivers drain into the Congo. This vast rolling basin is surrounded by steep plateaus and mountains, forming its rim.

The Congo River

The Congo River is the second-longest river in Africa, shorter only than the Nile River in Egypt. It is the seventh-longest river in the world. It is also quite wide, approximately 6 miles (10 km) wide at the midpoint of its length. Because it is so wide and deep, only one river, the Amazon, in South America, carries more water. Throughout the course of its 2,718 miles (4,373 km) it forms much of the border between the Democratic Republic of the Congo and the Republic of the Congo before emptying into the Atlantic Ocean. Along the way, hundreds of tributary rivers join it, covering an area more than one-third the size of the United States.

The area in which the rivers join the Congo is called the Congo River basin. It includes nearly all of Congo, the Republic of the Congo, part of Zambia, the Central African Republic, and northern Angola. Many rivers feed into the Congo, including the Kasai and the Lomami Rivers to the south, and the Aruwimi and Ubangi Rivers to the north. Boyoma Falls along the Congo River spills one of the world's largest annual volumes of water.

The Congo's path is unusual in that it flows in a large arc north and south of the equator. These sides alternate wet and dry seasons, allowing the river to pick up a regular supply of water year-round. The amount of water flowing in the river remains constant. This baffled early explorers before they had studied the entire length of the river. Until they understood its unusual path, they couldn't explain why its flow didn't decrease during the dry season.

The Congo River plays an important part in the country's transportation system. Because much of the interior of Congo is heavily forested and lightly populated, there are few roads. Most people and cargo enter the interior by boat, using the river and its tributaries. On this water system there are about 7,200 navigable miles (11,585 km) within the country.

As they slowly drop in altitude, they fall inward in slopes and steps like that of a huge stadium. It covers some 1.6 million square miles (4.1 million square kilometers). Much of this land is wet and swampy, though there are heavily forested areas of dry, firm land as well.

The soil here is called equatorial soil, which is soil found in warm, moist places. Plentiful rains assure that the soil is well covered with lush plant life. Because little erosion occurs here, the soil remains fixed, or stays in place. Much of it is soft and swampy due to decaying plant material. Over the years it has built up a thick layer of soft humus, organic material that is created by decomposing plants and animals.

Thousands of years ago there was a great lake in the center of the basin, but it drained away as the mighty Congo cut through it. Now, the only remaining parts of that lake are Lake Tumba and Lake Mai-Ndombe, both located in the basin's west-central region.

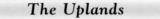

The Uplands

High plateaus edge the Congo basin at its northern and southern borders. In the north, these uplands are the Ubangi-Uele plateaus. Rising to heights as great as 4,000 feet (1,219 meters) they form the divide between the Congo River basin to their south and the Nile River basin to the north.

Several different plateaus and ranges form the southern border of the basin. In the southwest there is the Angola Plateau. Here, plateaus dominate the skyline. There is the Manikia Plateau, the high plains of Marungu, and the Bia and

Kibara Mountains. The highest points are found in the Kundelungu Plateau that rises to 5,250 feet (1,600 m) and in the Mitumba Plateau with heights reaching 4,921 feet (1,500 m).

Eastern Highlands

The mountains that form Congo's eastern highlands are a part of the Great Africa Rift. They extend north to south for more than 930 miles (1,500 km), from Lake Albert to south of Lubumbashi. The snow-capped Ruwenzori Mountains tower toward the sky at the equator and north. These are the tallest mountains in Congo. When missionaries saw these for the first time, they were amazed that snow could exist at the equator. Margherita Peak, with an elevation of 16,795 feet (5,119 m) is the nation's highest point. The Virunga Mountains, stretching across the Great Rift Valley, are just south of the Ruwenzori Mountains. They are volcanic and still spew smoke regularly out of their peaks.

Margherita Peak is the third-highest mountain in Africa. It was first climbed in 1906 by an Italian expedition and named for Queen Margherita of Italy.

Eruption!

In January 2002, Mount Nyiragongo in the Virunga Mountains erupted. The volcano ejected molten lava that nearly wiped out the city of Goma, killing more than forty people and causing hundreds of thousands to flee from their homes. Most returned, despite being warned of the dangers that awaited them. The water in Goma was contaminated, toxic sulfurous gases from the volcano remained in the air, and the volcano threatened to erupt again. Still, the people felt it was better to return home than to live in the poor conditions of the crowded refugee camps where they had to pay for water and where no food or medical treatment were available. Many camped nearby at the shores of polluted Lake Kivu. Six months later the volcano continued to rumble, but that did not stop the citizens of Goma who were working to rebuild their homes.

Nestled within these mountains are several large, beautiful lakes. Lake Tanganyika is the largest. South of it is Lake Mweru, and to the north are Lakes Kivu, Edward, and Albert. These lakes all help to form Congo's borders with the neighboring countries to the east.

Lake Tanganyika, the world's longest lake, is in many ways like the sea, except that it is not salty. It has been a source of food for locals with an abundance of fish.

Lakes Edward and Albert

Lake Edward (above), known in the Bantu language as *Edward Nyanza*, was named for Edward, prince of Wales. The lake is about 50 miles (80 km) long and 26 miles (42 km) wide. In 1889 Henry Morton Stanley was the first Western man to reach it. Stanley named the lake after the prince, who was born in 1841 to Queen Victoria. Edward VII became king of England, Scotland, and Ireland, when he was nearly sixty years old, in 1901. He and his wife, Alexandra of Denmark, were well regarded by their fellow citizens during Edward's rule, until his death in 1910.

Lake Albert, or *Albert Nyanza*, was named for Albert, prince consort of Britain. This lake, which, like Lake Edward, forms part of the boundary between Congo and Uganda, is about 100 miles (160 km) long, and 22 miles (35 km) wide. British explorer Sir Samuel Baker was the first European to see the lake, in 1864, and named it after the prince consort. Born in Germany in 1819, Albert married Queen Victoria in 1840, and, with her, had great influence on the politics, events, and arts of the time. He was only forty-two years old when he died of typhoid fever in 1861.

The soil in the eastern mountains is particularly rich. It has accumulated over centuries from the volcanic lava that covers some of the land. When the lava is finally broken down into soil, due to the effects of wind and rain, it becomes very fertile. This region has some of the best agricultural land in the country.

Congo's coastal strip is a narrow parcel of land, about 25 miles (40 m) wide, that follows the Congo River to the Atlantic Ocean. It is an area of low plains that head inland from the coast to the hill country of Mayumba and the Cristal Mountains. Mount Ula, the highest point in the Cristal Mountains, is 3,446 feet (1,050 m) above sea level.

The eastern area of the Congo is fertile due to the rich soil found there.

Congo's climate is generally tropical—warm and humid—with winds that are usually light. It is always under or near a low-pressure belt called the intertropical convergence zone (ITCZ), which hovers near the equator, shifting north and south with the seasons. The ITCZ causes masses of hot, moist tropical air from the Atlantic to rise and cool. This forms massive thunderclouds that roll over the land below. This weather system affects all of central Africa.

During the course of a twelve-month period, the ITCZ shifts from slightly north of the equator to just south of it, and then back northward again. The wettest time of the year for an area is when the ITCZ is over a region. Because the equator runs directly through the heart of the country, and the ITCZ crosses back and forth over it, it gets rain most of the year. From November through April the northern half of the country gets about 20 to 40 inches (50 to 100 centimeters) of rain, while the southern half gets 40 to 60 inches (100 to 150 cm). From May through October rains are still heavy at 20 to 40 inches (50 to 100 cm) through most of the country, especially the northern portion. Only parts of the southeastern Katanga have real dry seasons, which last four to five months.

Temperatures near the equator are usually warm year-round, day and

A Congolese family has a "taxi" push them across their flooded neighborhood in Kinshasa after heavy rains.

Congo's Geographical Features

Area of Country: 905,563 square miles (2,345,410 sq km)

Land and Water Borders: Republic of the Congo, Central African Republic, Sudan, Uganda, Rwanda, Burundi, Tanzania, Zambia, Angola, the Atlantic Ocean, Lake Tanganyika, the Congo River, Uele River, Ubangi River

Greatest Distance North to South: Approximately 1,300 miles (2,100 km)

Greatest Distance East to West: Approximately 1,200 miles (1,900 km)

Highest Elevation: Margherita Peak, 16,795 feet (5,119 m)

Lowest Elevation: Sea level

Length of Coastline: Approximately 25 miles (41 km)

Highest Average Temperature: 79°F (26.1°C) in January, Kinshasa

Lowest Average Temperature: 73°F (22.8°C) in July, Kinshasa

Average Annual Precipitation: 45 inches (1,143 mm), Kinshasa

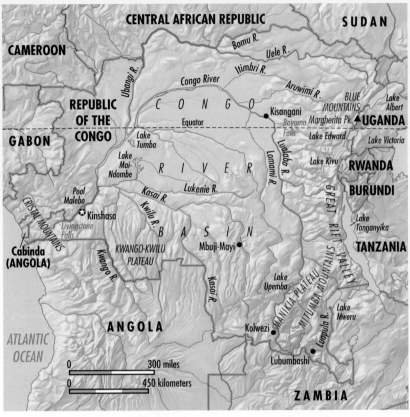

night. Most of Congo averages 70–80° Fahrenheit (21–27° Celsius) each month. It is slightly cooler in the higher altitudes of Congo's mountains, where the average annual temperature is around 66°F (19°C). However, temperatures vary little from day to day in each place. The city of Rananga, in southern Congo, has a difference of only about 3.5° from its warmest to its coolest months.

Looking at Congo's Cities

Lubumbashi (above), with 851,381 residents, is one of Congo's largest cities, second only to the capital of Kinshasa. Located in southeast Congo, near the border with Zambia, it is the capital of Katanga Province. Founded in 1910, Lubumbashi was first called Elisabethville. It immediately became a center for the region's copper-mining industry. Today copper is still smelted there. Other industries in Lubumbashi include printing, textiles, food and beverages, and brickmaking.

Mbuji-Mayi, formerly known as Bakwanga, is located in south-central Congo. It is the capital of the Kasai-Oriental Province, where the majority of the nation's diamonds are mined. Most of these diamonds are industrial grade and are used mainly for sanding and drilling. Nearly all of the industrial-grade diamonds in the world are mined here. In fact, the city was especially developed to be a center for diamond mining when it was established in 1910 by Europeans. Today it is home to some 806,475 Congolese.

Kolwezi, population 417,810, is located in Katanga Province. Copper and cobalt mining are the main industries here. Once the ore is mined, it is shipped east by rail for further processing. Kolwezi is also a center for trade of agricultural products grown nearby.

Kisangani (below) was founded in 1883 by the explorer Henry M. Stanley. It is the capital of Orientale Province, and a port on the Congo River in the north-central region of the country. Once known as Stanleyville, it's a hub of transportation on the Congo River and is also a manufacturing center for such products as furniture, beer, and metal goods. Its population is 417,517.

Congo's Bountiful Diversity

THANKS TO ITS GREAT DIVERSITY in landscape, Congo has more species of plants and animals than any other African nation. Congo is home to more than 400 types of mammals. No other country in Africa has more than 300. There are nearly 11,000 kinds of plants, and more than 3,000 of them grow only in Congo, mostly in the rain forest.

Tropical Rain Forest

Tropical rain forests, which surround the great Congo River and many of its tributaries, cover most of the Congo basin. These thick, lush forests are filled with several types of evergreens, trees that keep their leaves year-round. Many of these trees are more than 90 feet (28 m) tall, with some as tall as 160 feet (52 m). Buttress roots support the trees by growing up from the soil to the trunk to prop it up. These tall trees, called emergent trees, form a canopy, or upper layer of plant life in the rain forest. Smaller trees that thrive in a shady environment make up the growth below the canopy. Mahogany, iroko, limba, rubber, palm, and ebony are some of the trees growing here.

Rain forests in the central and northern regions of the Congo make up nearly half of the country's total area.

Opposite: **Virunga National Park's wetlands are home to hippos, whose population has been sharply decreasing due to war and poachers.**

An abundance of ferns grow in Congo's rain forests.

Lianas are climbing vines found in rain forests. Their thick, woody stems begin life on the forest floor, but depend on trees for support as they climb upward.

Ferns grow in the moisture collected on trees, and flowering, woody vines called lianas climb up the trunks. There is a shrub layer here, too, with small trees, ferns, and palms. Sisal and raffia, fibrous mid-sized plants that are often used for weaving, are found along the rain forest floor. Additional plants thrive at ground level, including edible mushrooms and African violets that prosper in the poor light and rich soil. Lilies and bird-of-paradise plants are found here, too.

Forest-Savanna Mosaic

The forest-savanna mosaic has a two-part name because of its unusual nature. It is land that was once rain forest, but is now, in many places, a grassy savanna. Humans caused this change in the land. Trees were cut in order to clear land for grazing cattle and growing crops. Rain forest trees that were once common to the whole area now grow mostly near rivers. Most of this area, though, is simply low grassland and meadow. The land is often burned by the farmers so that the old plants die, and new, tender plants sprout for grazing. A few trees such, as coconut palms and banana, are cultivated, grown by farmers, and produce valuable fruits. Farmers also raise tobacco and coffee plants.

Fruit trees, such as the banana, are grown by farmers in Congo.

The wooded savanna is found high in Congo's northern and southern uplands. Even though the summers are wet there, the winter season is long and dry, so plants growing there must be able to do well in these harsh conditions. Only a few trees can manage. The baobab trees, for example, with their thick trunks, survive the drought and live there along with woody shrubs and tall, wiry grasses.

Mountainous Forest

Congo's mountainous region is a thin strip along its eastern border. Plant life varies here, depending upon how high up the mountain a plant grows. At elevations above 15,000 feet (4,500 m) there is only snow. At 12,000 to 15,000 feet (3,600 to 4,500 m), is the subalpine zone. Not much grows here except for scrubby plants, clumps of grass that cover the ground, woody shrubs, and flowering lobelias.

Dwarf woodlands, at 10,000 to 12,000 feet (3,000 to 3,600 m), are drier, and therefore brighter, than the misty regions below. A variety of plants and small trees grow nicely here, including woody shrubs and other green, leafy plants. Just below is a band of tall mountain bamboo, at altitudes of about 8,000 to 10,000 feet (2,400 to 3,000 m).

Tropical forests grow at elevations of 6,000 to 8,000 feet (1,800 to 2,400 m). Tree ferns are common here, as well as tall trees that make up the canopy. Shrubs and ground covers thrive below the canopy, filling the forest with plant life.

The dampest part of the mountain forest is at about 6,000 feet (1,800 m). This is where the cloud layer is, and mist hangs

Covered in clouds and mist, plant life in the moist mountainous forest grows heavy with mosses and lichens.

in the air. The trees are constantly wet, so mosses and lichens can exist on them. Beautiful orchids grow well in this environment, too.

Animal Life in the Rain Forest

Many types of wild animals live in Congo. Just like plants, animal species vary from region to region. They live in the environment most capable of meeting their needs for food, water, and shelter. On the ground, several large mammals forage

Though the okapi is related to the giraffe, it does not stand nearly as tall; it is about 5 feet (1.5 m) tall.

for food These include the okapi, a rare animal that is related to the giraffe but looks much more like a cow. The only place it lives is Congo, and many consider it a symbol of the country. Other mammals include antelopes such as bongos and duikers. There are also elephant shrews, which are small insect-eaters, leopards, and forest genets, which look something like cats.

Elephant shrews get their name from their long snouts, which they can move about much like an elephant can his trunk!

The red colobus is one of the most endangered monkeys in the world. They survive on leaves, fruit, flowers, and stems.

Some primates stay mostly on the ground, including lowland gorillas, chimpanzees, and pygmy chimpanzees, which are found only in Congo. Other primates live higher up in the vegetation, swinging through the canopy in search of food. These include galagos, which are also known as bush babies, and red colobus monkeys.

Birds of the rain forest include hornbills, parrots, crowned eagles, and Congo peacocks, all of which add color and sound to the setting.

Several types of snakes make their homes throughout the rain forest, slinking across the ground or slithering up a tree. These include poisonous vipers and mambas, as well as pythons, all of which prey on small mammals. Butterflies and giant beetles are two of the many insects of the rain forest.

Though savanna lands are often used for agriculture, farmers have avoided raising large livestock, because large farm animals such as cows are vulnerable to the tsetse fly. The poisonous bite of this nasty pest can cause sleeping sickness in humans and is also often deadly for domesticated cattle. It's not a threat to wild animals, though, many of which have made their homes on these open grasslands. Plant-eating mammals do particularly well here, because they rarely face a shortage of food. Zebras, antelopes, black and white rhinoceroses, giraffes,

Zebras make their home on the savanna grasslands. They graze on grass, leaves, bark, roots, and stems.

buffalo, and elephants are some of the large animals, while smaller animals include rhebock, tiny oribi, aardvarks, baboons, and warthogs. A few predatory mammals live here, including African wildcats, known as servals, cheetahs, hyenas, jackals, wild dogs, and leopards.

Vultures and eagles fly across the savanna's broad skyline. Secretary birds eat insects. There are also reptiles, such as the agama lizard. At the beginning of the savanna's rainy season, butterflies take to the air, painting the sky with their great numbers.

Animals of the Mountains

The mountains on Congo's eastern border provide a habitat unlike any other in the country. Though it's only a thin strip of land, the diversity of animals here is surprising. The most famous animal of the Congo, the mountain gorilla, is an endangered species living only in the Virunga Mountains, at altitudes of around 11,000 feet (3,400 m).

In the Ruwenzori Range, at altitudes of around 9,000 to 10,000 feet (2,700 to 3,000 m), chimpanzees swing from the trees. They share this habitat with some unusual creatures, including the miniature-sized forest elephants, which are only about two-thirds the size of regular African elephants. The buffalo here are small, too, just half the size of buffalo found on the savannas. Colobus monkeys live farther up the mountainside at the subalpine level of about 12,000 to 15,000 feet (3,600 to 4,500 m). Birds in the mountainous region include hornbills and the colorful crested turacos.

The Mountain Gorilla

Mountain gorillas are the world's largest primates, with females weighing around 220 pounds (100 kilograms) and males weighing an average of 352 pounds (160 kg). Their thick bodies are accented with long, muscular arms, large heads, and short legs. Their long silky coats are shades of black or brown.

Despite their fearsome size and appearance, gorillas are usually very gentle and intelligent. They spend about 30 percent of each day feeding on grasses, roots, leaves, and stems of bamboo and other shrubs. Another 30 percent of the day is used by traveling throughout their territory and 40 percent at rest.

The average life of a male mountain gorilla is fifty years. Females typically live forty years and have two to six offspring during that time. Babies are nursed for three years, and their mothers continue to care for them for several years beyond that.

Today, mountain gorillas are a highly endangered species. Poachers face severe penalties for killing the wild animals illegally, but the killing goes on anyway. Gorilla heads, hands, and feet are highly prized by collectors. Fighting that is going on in the Virunga Mountains where they live also contributes to their deaths when the gorillas are caught in the crossfire. Also, authorities are hesitant to enter the region to stop poachers. In addition, they are losing their habitat to farming and logging.

Water Animals

Many animals of Congo make their homes in or near water, whether it be rivers, lakes, or the Atlantic Ocean. The Congo River and its tributaries are home to many interesting creatures, including several aquatic mammals. Hippopotamuses wallow in its waters, as do swamp otters. Some of the reptiles and amphibians here are dwarf crocodiles and dwarf water frogs, freshwater turtles, and sedge frogs.

The dwarf crocodile can be found in fresh water streams, rivers, and wetlands. It grows up to 5 to 6 feet and weighs as little as 40 pounds to 70 pounds.

A male saddlebill stork plucks a frog from the water to eat.

Freshwater fish include tiger fish and tilapia, the colorful jewel-like cichlid, the capitaine, catfish, eels, and electric fish. Unusual fish are the African lungfish and the bichir, which are primitive-looking and bony. These fish are often food for the birds of Congo's waterways. Several types of stork, including the saddlebill stork, eat fish and frogs, while African eagles prey upon fish.

Reptiles are found in Congo's lakes and rivers. There are some dangerous snakes, such as vipers, tree cobras, and pythons. Chameleons and salamanders are common, too.

Problems Facing Congo's Wildlife

Many of Congo's wild animals are fighting for their survival. They face several threats that could possibly wipe out entire species from the region. Every day the rain forest is cleared by loggers and farmers who want the land for growing crops. This loss of habitat is devastating to animals, which are no longer able to find the food and shelter they need. Many die. Sometimes animals such as chimpanzees are captured alive, to be sold to people who want exotic pets.

But the bigger problem facing wildlife is hunting and war. War strips animals of their safe places to live. Elephants, okapi, gorillas, and rhinos, in particular, are losing their lives as they lose their habitat.

Garamba Park, in northeast Congo, was home to about 12,000 elephants, but since 1998, when rebel fighters began hiding out in the park, approximately 1,000 elephants have died each year. The entire elephant population of 350 has been wiped out in Kahuzi-Biega National Park. There used to be 280 lowland gorillas in that park in 1996, but half of them were killed within five years.

Hunting is strictly regulated, but people who are starving break the laws to kill animals for food. Both lowland and mountain gorillas are eaten by soldiers in the field. Okapi are also slaughtered, and rare apes, bonobos (below), are popular food in the bush. Bonobos, it turns out, are tasty and cheaper than beef. They are sold illegally to people living in cities. The bonobo population in Congo was about 100,000 in 1980, but there were fewer than 3,000 left twenty years later.

Kingdoms,
Colonies, and
Corruption

CONGO'S HISTORY BEGINS LONG BEFORE THE TIME WHEN people kept track of it by recording historical events. We know very little about what life was like for the first people who lived in Congo. We do know that some lived in the jungle where there were plenty of resources, and dangers as well. They faced challenges every day just to stay alive. That part of life in Congo hasn't changed much. Those living there, from prehistoric times until today, have had to deal with many difficulties. They continue to struggle to make a better life for themselves.

Opposite: **Societies have lived in the Congo as long ago as 10,000 B.C. Migrations beginning about 1,000 B.C. spread cultures throughout the Congo.**

The Earliest People

During prehistoric times, Pygmies were the first people to live in the region that is now Congo. All the resources they needed to survive were found in the jungle. There were plants offering fruits and vegetables, and animals for protein. The frames of their shelters were made from sticks tied together with vines and roofs made of leaves. They were nomadic, meaning that they moved about. When one area no longer had enough resources to fill their needs, they journeyed to a new home.

About 2,000 years ago Pygmies were joined by Bantu-speaking people from the north. They spread east and south throughout the area, introducing farming. Palm trees and yams were among their first crops. Later, newcomers from the Sudan region brought with them cattle-herding practices.

Pygmies

"Pygmies" is a term loosely applied to a human sub-group noted for their short stature, which is an inherited trait. Most adult males grow only to an average height of 59 inches (1.5 m). Today, Pygmies live not only in Congo, but are scattered from Camaroon to Rwanda and southwestern Africa, as well as in parts of India, New Guinea, and the Malay Peninsula. Many follow traditional hunting and gathering practices, while others have adapted to a more modern lifestyle, living as farmers.

Congolese Pygmies now inhabit one of the country's most remote regions, the Ituri Forest, living the way they have lived for thousands of years. The best known tribe of Pygmies in Congo are the Bambuti, the shortest among all the world's ethnic groups. Adults average only about 51 inches (130 cm) in height.

They also grew grains. More people brought banana-growing techniques, while other newcomers shared their knowledge of making tools from iron and copper.

This additional knowledge made it possible for people to settle in one area and provide for themselves. As they settled,

This illustration shows a Congolese village and trading post.

they set up social structures based on family. Some had higher rankings than others within the group. There were people who were rulers, some who enforced laws, and others who did the work. By 1500 most of Congo was arranged into several complex kingdoms.

Kingdoms of Congo

One of the earliest kingdoms to be established was the Kongo Kingdom, during the 1300s. It went on to become one of the strongest as well. The original Kongo people lived around the mouth of the Congo River, but the kingdom eventually

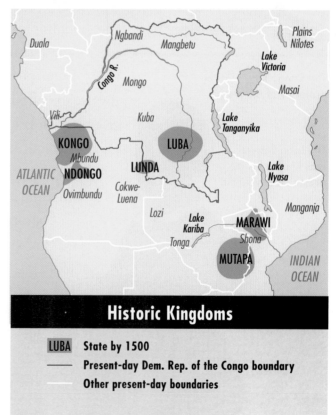

Historic Kingdoms

LUBA State by 1500
—— Present-day Dem. Rep. of the Congo boundary
—— Other present-day boundaries

The Kongo king was the protector of the people.

The Luba Empire was known for its artistic achievement.

covered the region from what is currently north-west Angola to Gabon. Other important kingdoms included the Luba and the Lunda empires to the east and Azande in the northeast, but there were many more throughout the region. Though each was different, all had central authority figures, often with lesser rulers helping to run the kingdom.

This system worked mostly peacefully as it developed throughout Congo. Each kingdom developed special characteristics, and its own forms of culture and religion. The Kongo Kingdom, for example, was the largest. Lunda was known for its successful and complex system of government. The Luba people, who believed their king had divine powers, excelled at art and music. Occasionally, different groups within kingdoms fought for power. These battles, though sometimes fierce, rarely lasted long or went outside the kingdom. There were some skirmishes between kingdoms, but again, these were usually minor and short-lived.

Europeans Arrive

Late in 1482 Portuguese navigators arrived. As their ships sailed over the horizon toward Africa, it appeared to the Kongo people on land that the ships were rising from the spirit world below. The beings that got off the ships were white. The locals thought they had been drained of all their color, which is what they believed happened to people who entered the spirit world. It was an amazing and frightening experience for the Kongo people, but they treated the Portuguese kindly.

The Portuguese were impressed with the many riches the Kongo Kingdom held. The Portuguese soon realized that the kingdom's resources, especially ivory, could bring great wealth to them. More Portuguese soon arrived. The Kongo people established a working relationship with the Portuguese and supplied them with goods. The Portuguese, in return, introduced Christianity to the locals, provided them with tools and goods from Europe, and later introduced corn, tobacco, and cassava crops to the region.

The Congo was one of the main sources of slaves for Arabia, the Middle East, and the New World. Many times, African merchants brought slaves to coastal trading posts.

By the early 1500s the Portuguese increasingly concentrated on slave trading. Slaves were very valuable as they were needed to work on plantations in the West Indies and the Americas. At first the Kongo people assisted in capturing people, often entire families, from other kingdoms of the Congo region. They were sold to the Portuguese. Soon other Europeans became involved

in the slave trade. The Kongo people made a lot of money doing this, but they became extremely cruel.

The Kongo Kingdom grew wealthy from the slave trade, but it also became the target of great anger from other kingdoms, whose people were forced to become slaves. Conflict developed with the Portuguese, who then shifted their slave-trading operations to Angola. By the time Kongo was attacked by groups of warriors from the Jaga people to the east, it had become weak. Later the Luba and Lunda kingdoms, also involved in capturing other black Africans and selling them as slaves, were also attacked.

Because of the slave trade, the region was in disarray. Money and power were in the hands of a few, and once-strong kingdoms were powerless. Kingdoms were fighting among each other, and, because the Europeans had introduced firearms, battles were more ferocious than ever. All of this happened within a few hundred years. People who had once coexisted peacefully were torn apart. The time was ripe for a takeover, and King Leopold II of Belgium just happened to be ready, too.

The King and the Congo

Leopold II was the king of Belgium. Belgium is a fairly small European country, and King Leopold felt frustrated by this. He observed other European countries colonizing various parts of the world—England had India and chunks of north and west Africa. He decided Belgium needed to have a colony in some part of the world, too. But many of the best places were already taken. Where could Belgium have a colony?

At the Berlin Conference in 1884, King Leopold II was allowed to take over and claim the Congo, as long as he bettered the people and the country. However, he exploited the people and forced them into hard labor.

Henry Morton Stanley

Henry Morton Stanley was the most important explorer of Congo. The work he accomplished there, on behalf of King Leopold II, changed the nation forever.

He was born in Wales in 1841, and originally was named John Rowlands. At age sixteen he came to the United States and took the name of his adoptive father, who lived in New Orleans, Louisiana. Shortly afterward the Civil War began, and Stanley took a turn at fighting for each side, but soon discovered he was meant for journalism.

He worked for several newspapers, following wars and explorations and chronicling his adventures for the people back home. When missionary/explorer David Livingstone was thought to be lost while traveling throughout Africa, the *New York Herald* hired Stanley to find him and to write about it along the way. Stanley uttered those famous words, "Dr. Livingstone, I presume?" when he found his man on the shores of Lake Tanganyika, in 1871. A few years later Stanley led an exploration himself, following the Congo River from midcourse to the sea. He tried to entice British leaders with stories of the land surrounding the river, but few were impressed. Yet King Leopold II was a willing listener and ready to begin developing the area. The king sponsored Stanley on yet another exploration to Congo, from 1879 to 1884, and Stanley helped the king get rights to the land. America's support for King Leopold II at the time came in part at Stanley's urging. He made one more trip to the Congo and then spent his later years writing about his life. He died in 1904. He had been a very influential man.

This question was quickly answered by Henry Morton Stanley, who explored the Congo from 1874 to 1877. No other European had ever traveled so far up the Congo River—they stopped when the rapids and hilly terrain made it too difficult. But Stanley persevered and trekked the entire length of the river. He returned home to Great Britain with tales of the country's vast and bountiful interior, urging the government to colonize Congo. But Britain wasn't interested. Here was Leopold's chance to form a colony!

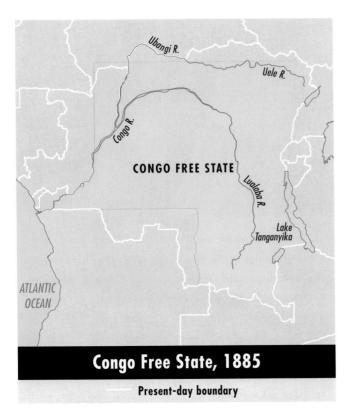

Congo Free State, 1885

Present-day boundary

In 1885 Leopold created the Congo Free State, his name for Congo. It looked to all the world as if it were a Belgian colony created for the betterment of Congolese people. They were to be educated and receive medical care, Leopold said, but these were lies. The Congo Free State actually was owned by King Leopold himself, who had tricked some 450 native kings and chiefs into giving up their land.

Leopold's men forced the Congolese people to work. They were taken from their homes and families and made to build roads and railroads. Roadways, railroads, and shipping on the Congo River were needed to carry the great resources from the country's vast interior to the ocean, where it could be shipped away. There was ivory from elephants and rubber from rubber trees. Rubber had only recently become an important resource, for cars had just been invented and rubber was in demand for tires. Thousands of men, women, and even children were forced into labor. They had to kill elephants and haul the ivory; they had to tap rubber trees and carry the sap. They were poorly fed and forced to march with heavy loads for hundreds of miles. If they quit or complained, they were tortured or shot. Many times their hands or fingers were chopped

The Congo produced a vast amount of rubber in 1906. In this illustration, Congolese find the value of their loads.

off. Leopold quickly branched into the slave trade, and the Congo River became a pipeline for slaves. His men, and some natives who joined them, traveled far upriver and rounded up entire villages. The villagers were defenseless against European guns.

Leopold's history in Congo is marked by great physical violence and brutality. He viewed the people of Congo as if they were another resource, not much different from elephants' ivory. For years the world paid little attention, but, slowly, missionaries and merchants began to share with the world the terrible things they had witnessed in Congo. Eventually there was an international uproar, particularly from Great Britain and the United States.

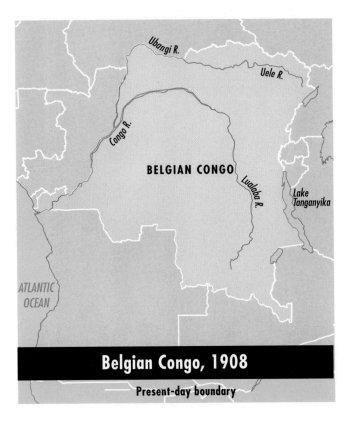

Belgian Congo, 1908

Present-day boundary

In order to stop the outcry, in 1908 the Belgian parliament voted to annex Congo and make it a colony. This took Congo out of Leopold's direct rule. The Congo Free State was renamed the Belgian Congo. The Belgians, as colonists, were far less severe, but still treated the Congolese as inferior. They imposed high taxes and made villagers give a portion of their crops to the government each year.

Congolese troops, along with Allied troops, fought in World War I (1914–1918). They helped to conquer German East Africa, which is now Rwanda and Burundi, while the British got the rest. After the war, life improved for the Congolese people. The Belgian colonists still looked down upon them, but were more generous, improving health care and education and providing better-paying jobs.

During World War II Belgium tapped into the Congo's many natural resources to help pay for Belgium's contribution to the Allied Forces. More and more rural Congolese moved to the country's urban areas for the jobs that were being created there. As they gathered, they began to call for reforms in the way they were governed. Eventually the Congolese were allowed to own land and participate in local politics. These freedoms made the people hungry for more.

The Alliance of the Kongo People (ABAKO) called for immediate independence in 1956. Soon they were joined by other groups of native people. The following year the Congolese people were allowed to elect local city councils, and members of ABAKO won most of these seats in the capital city of Kinshasa. When Belgians tried to ban a Kinshasa political meeting in January 1959, rioting followed. The Congolese people were tired of waiting for independence.

In 1960, after the details of independence had been worked out at the Round Table Conference in Brussels,

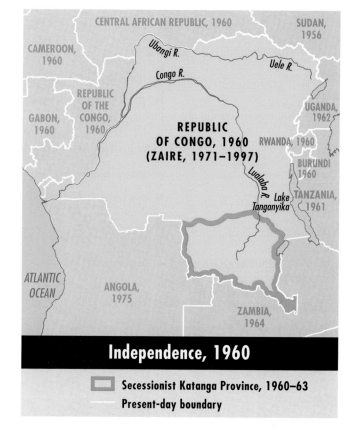

Independence, 1960

☐ Secessionist Katanga Province, 1960–63
— Present-day boundary

Congolese delegates appear at the Round Table Conference where deliberations took place for the country's independence.

Belgium, they got their wish. The new country, named the Republic of Congo, was established on June 30, 1960. Patrice Lumumba, who led the largest organization fighting for independence, was elected prime minister, and Joseph Kasavubu, president. One of Lumumba's aides, Joseph-Désiré Mobutu, was chosen to head the military.

Patrice Lumumba

Born in 1925, Patrice Lumumba was educated at missionary schools and then entered civil service. In the 1950s independence movements in neighboring countries inspired him to help Congo work toward its own independence. He made speeches, wrote articles, and tried to unite people around the cause. In 1958 he founded the Congolese National Movement (MNC), the first nationwide Congolese political party. Lumumba envisioned a united Congo with a strong central government. Others, including Joseph Kasavubu, wanted a federal system, with power divided among territories.

Following national elections in 1960, Lumumba became prime minister and Kasavubu became president. But the country quickly fell apart. In the trouble that followed, Kasavubu dismissed Lumumba. Military leader Mobutu took control of the country, and Lumumba was captured. He was assassinated on January 17, 1961.

Today Lumumba is remembered as a hero by his followers and even by those who were opposed to him. His ideas, as expressed in a farewell letter to his wife, live on. He wrote: "The only thing we wanted for our country was the right to a decent existence, to dignity without hypocrisy, to independence without restrictions. The day will come when history will have its say."

The new country faced many problems. The economy suffered, as many European business owners fled the country. Public services were limited. The army was weak, and the many diverse ethnic groups could not reach agreements on issues. Violent conflicts erupted throughout the country. In addition, Katanga Province, then known as Shaba, threatened to leave Congo and form its own country. Lumumba and Kasavubu disagreed on the role of the United Nations in stopping the violence. Kasavubu fired Lumumba, then Mobutu quickly led a successful military coup, or takeover, and finally, in 1965, Mobutu took complete control of the country.

Mobutu led the country for more than thirty years, until 1997. His reign will be remembered for the harsh control he held over Congo, and the personal wealth he seized while the country fell into deep poverty. He claimed to make the country become more authentically African by changing the names of people, cities, and even the country to traditional African names. Thus *Congo* became *Zaire* in 1971, which was actually an old Portuguese name. He changed his own name to Mobutu Sese Seko.

Though several groups wanted to get rid of Mobutu, he and his army were able to stop all opposition. He allowed many foreign investors into the country to profit from its resources. In return, he enjoyed good relations with world leaders who helped support his presidency.

His opposition, however, continued to grow. Congolese people were angry with Mobutu for numerous reasons. The country's economy was a mess and they were hungry. They did not have the right to choose their leaders. Fights between the nation's various ethnic groups were growing, too, as different groups fought to control valuable resources. By 1990 Mobutu's international popularity was falling. To keep foreign leaders happy, he vowed to bring democracy to Congo. Though several attempts were made to write a new constitution that would give people greater freedom, Mobutu and his people managed to block any advances.

In the early 1990s terrible fighting broke out in Rwanda and Uganda between two ethnic groups, the Hutus and the Tutsis. More than a million refugees from that conflict poured into Congo in 1994 alone. Additional refugees came from Burundi, Angola, and Sudan. All were trying to escape the violence and bloodshed in their homelands. But they couldn't escape. There was violence in Congo then, too, between government forces and rebels trying to overthrow them. Most of those refugees, nearly 900,000 of them, chose or were forced to return home in 1996. About 200,000 refugees from Rwanda were never accounted for. Many believe that they were killed by forces in Congo.

As the ethnic fighting and the war over resources grew, so did anger at Mobutu. Troops and rebel forces from Rwanda, Uganda, and Burundi took over great portions of Congo, killing citizens or forcing them to flee in fear. Beginning in October 1996, a group called the Alliance of Democratic Forces for the Liberation of Congo, led by Laurent Kabila, fought Mobutu's forces for six months, with help from Rwanda and Uganda. They took control of the government in May

1997, and Mobutu stepped down. Kabila renamed the country the Democratic Republic of the Congo and declared himself president.

Congolese people greeted him with high hopes but quickly were disappointed. Kabila's policies did little to end the fighting or the poverty. Unrest continued to grow, as some seven or eight different factions fought in Congo. Battles were especially heavy in the eastern part of the nation, where many of the valuable mineral resources are found. Civil war broke out, as some fighting groups tried to get rid of Kabila's government. Neighboring countries quickly took sides and joined in. Uganda and Rwanda backed the rebels, while troops from Angola, Namibia, and Zimbabwe supported the government.

During the late 1990s the people of then Zaire, believed Laurent Kabila would free them from the dictatorship of Mobutu Sese Seko. However, Kabila's policies did not regain peace and a new war began.

Early in 2001 Kabila was assassinated by one of his own bodyguards. His son Joseph, only 29 years old, replaced him as president. He has shown a greater willingness to work to end the war, participating in peace talks with Rwanda. A tentative peace agreement was reached in September 2002, but fighting continued. Hundreds of civilians were massacred in ethnic conflicts in April 2003. Most observers agree that a lasting peace will be hard to achieve.

Moving Toward Freedom

Despite its name, the Democratic Republic of the Congo is not democratic. Citizens have no choice in their government. For decades the nation was a dictatorship, with one man making all the decisions. Congo now has a government in transition. Since 1990 it has been moving—slowly—toward giving its citizens the freedom to choose their leaders.

The reforms began when world leaders grew increasingly angry with President Mobutu Sese Seko and his corrupt government. Powerful countries like the United States began to withhold aid, so Mobutu knew changes had to be made. A democratic, multiparty system would be created, he announced in 1990. Today, such a government still does not exist in Congo.

A conference to write a new constitution collapsed in disarray in 1991. Rescheduled for early 1992, the conference was shut down again—this time by Mobutu's government. Finally, in 1993, delegates at a conference produced a new constitution and created an interim government. But Mobutu refused to give up his own power. Chaos and confusion followed, and the process to bring democracy to the country came to a halt.

When Mobutu was forced from power in 1997, Laurent Kabila declared himself president. He promised a new constitution in 1998 and free elections in 1999. But Kabila and the others on his leadership team were inexperienced and unable

Opposite: **Congolese soldiers march at the national football stadium to celebrate the anniversary of the overthrow of Mobutu Sese Seko.**

Mobutu Sese Seko

Mobutu Sese Seko led the Congo from 1965 until 1997. Congo's current government is working to change many of his policies; however, the things he did during his long regime shaped the country greatly.

Mobutu was born in the north of what was then the Belgian Congo in 1930 and was named Joseph Désiré Mobutu. He attended missionary schools, and in 1956 joined the Congolese National Movement led by Patrice Lumumba. As a onetime member of the Belgian colonial army, Mobutu had quickly risen in rank to the highest position open to black men, sergeant major, but had left that position to pursue a career in journalism. When the country achieved independence in 1960, Lumumba became prime minister and named Mobutu army chief of staff.

There was much turmoil over how the country should be governed. In 1960 Mobutu led a coup, or an attempted takeover, of the country which led to the assassination of Lumumba. At first Mobutu settled for a behind-the-scenes role of "strongman." But in 1965 he simply abolished civilian rule and declared himself president. He canceled the elections that were to be held the next year and created the Popular Movement of the Revolution as the country's only political party. All citizens had to join. In the 1970 presidential election, Mobutu was the only candidate. He ran unopposed and won.

One of his first actions was to change the name of the country to Zaire, which he felt was more African and authentic. Several city names were changed. The capital of Leopoldville, for example, became Kinshasa. He ordered the Congolese people to change their

European names to African names. He changed his own name to Mobutu Sese Seko Kuku Ngbendu wa za Banga, which, translated, supposedly means "the all-powerful warrior who, because of his endurance and inflexible will to win, will go from conquest to conquest leaving fire in his wake." Some people felt that his desire to return his country to its African roots helped bring unity to the many ethnic groups in the Congo. But he also did a lot of damage. He forced out foreign business owners and turned the businesses over to locals, who often did not know how to run them properly. Mobutu refused to let anyone disagree with him, and frequently killed those who did. He took the country's wealth as his own, sharing it only with those closest to him. The rest of the country was stuck in dire poverty.

The United States and many other nations initially supported him, but eventually cut aid to the country because of Mobutu's corruption as well as the government's. The country's army remained weak, and so it was unable to stop the revolt by ethnic rebels from the eastern part of the country. Laurent Kabila led this group, which took over the country in May 1997. Mobutu went into exile in Morocco, and died a few months later.

to pull off such sweeping changes in such a short time. A new constitution had not yet been drafted when Kabila was assassinated in 2001. His son, Joseph, was appointed president. Under his guidance, Congo's struggle for democracy and freedom has continued to inch forward. A new power-sharing constitution was signed in the spring of 2003, but great changes seem unlikely as long as warring factions remain unreconciled.

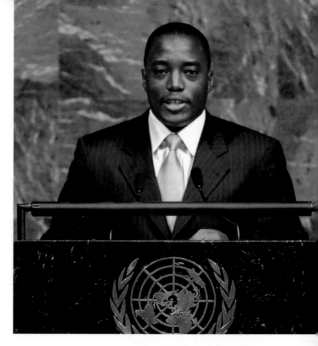

Democratic Republic of the Congo president Joseph Kabila addresses the UN General Assembly at the UN headquarters in New York City.

Structure of the Government

The transitional government in Congo is a republic. Much of the authority and power is centered in the president, who is head of the government and chief of state. He appoints a twenty-five-member cabinet, called the National Executive Council. He also appoints people to the 300-member Transitional Constitutional Assembly, based in Lubumbashi. There are ten provinces in the country, each led by a provincial governor, who is also appointed by the president. There is a supreme court in Congo. Laws in the country are based on two traditions: tribal law and the Belgian civil law system.

Members of the Supreme Court look on as Joseph Kabila (fourth from the left) takes the oath of office in January 2001.

NATIONAL GOVERNMENT OF THE DEMOCRATIC REPUBLIC OF THE CONGO

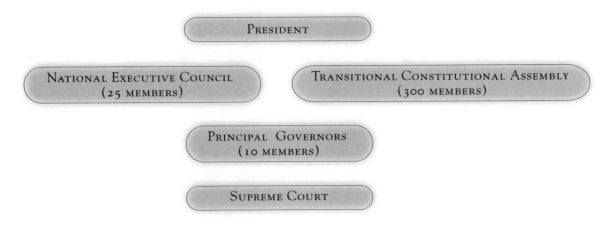

PRESIDENT

NATIONAL EXECUTIVE COUNCIL
(25 MEMBERS)

TRANSITIONAL CONSTITUTIONAL ASSEMBLY
(300 MEMBERS)

PRINCIPAL GOVERNORS
(10 MEMBERS)

SUPREME COURT

President Kabila has led the country further toward democracy. He has eased the laws restricting political parties and promotes greater human rights. But Congo faces many problems: war, poverty, and disease. These issues affect people in the most basic way. They truly mean the difference between life and death. Before the struggle for democracy can become the most important topic in Congo, these immense problems must be solved.

National Flag

The flag of the Democratic Republic of the Congo has a large gold star in the center of a plain blue field and a line of six small stars on the left edge. The flag has some historical significance. The design was from the flag of the Congo Free State in 1877. It symbolized the nation as the shining light in the "Dark Continent," as Africa was popularly known at the time. When the country gained its independence in 1960, the six small stars were added to represent the six provinces that existed at the time. In 1971, then-president Mobutu

Sese Seko changed the flag to a green field, depicting an arm carrying a torch. But when Laurent Kabila came to power in 1997, his regime restored the old flag.

Kinshasa: Did You Know This?

Kinshasa, with a population of 6,050,000, is capital of the Democratic Republic of the Congo. Kinshasa is the largest city in Congo and growing rapidly. This is because the government concentrates most of its spending on its capital city, attracting people from other cities. People are also drawn to the city's culture, sports, music, and employment opportunities. A high birth rate adds to the population, as well.

Several museums are located here, including the National Museum of Kinshasa, which holds fascinating archaeological finds from the region. There are two universities in Kinshasa, the University of Kinshasa and the University of Ambakart. There is a zoo, a large sports stadium, and a Roman Catholic cathedral.

When Henry Morton Stanley was exploring Congo at the request of King Leopold II, he came upon what is now Kinshasa. In 1881, he renamed it Leopoldville, in honor of the king. It replaced Boma as the capital of the Belgian Congo in 1926. When Mobutu changed the names of several cities after the country regained its independence, Leopoldville was named Kinshasa. It is the name of one of the villages that had been on the spot back in 1881.

Kinshasa receives 45 inches (114 cm) of rainfall each year. The average daily temperature in January is 79°F (26.1°C), while in July it is 73°F (22.8°C).

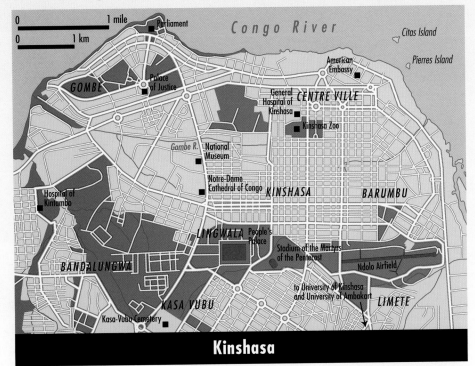

Kinshasa

Poverty Amid Plenty

DIAMONDS ARE CONGO'S MOST FLASHY AND FAMOUS natural resource, but there are many more. It is a nation graced with many valuable plants, animals, and minerals. It is centrally located on the continent and is in a good position to trade with other African nations. Congo also has ocean access, providing the opportunity to ship products around the world. While Congo's tremendous resources give it the potential to be a wealthy country—perhaps even one of Africa's richest—its people are, in fact, very poor.

Decades of colonization and corrupt leadership have taken their toll. Other countries, and many individuals, have made fortunes from Congo's resources, but most Congolese live in poverty. More than 16 million people, nearly a third of the population, live in severe poverty. There are more than 2 million homeless people as well. Many international aid organizations have declared Congo to have the worst humanitarian crisis in the world.

Opposite: **A diamond miner examines a sieve for gems at a jungle diamond mine. Miners live an insecure life as they wait for the next big stone.**

A Congolese fisherman sits outside his home in Kinshasa along the Congo River. More than 15 million Congolese live in poverty.

Congolese Currency

The basic unit of currency in Congo is the Congolese franc. A franc is divided into 100 makuta. Many different scenes are shown on the banknotes. The 50-franc note depicts an ethnic Chokwe mask. Other notes show such scenes as an elephant, a Congo River valley, and a hydroelectric dam.

As of October 2003, one Congolese franc was worth less than three-tenths of one cent in U.S. dollars. It would take more than 422 Congolese francs to equal one U.S. dollar.

The Causes of Congo's Poverty

The political troubles the country has endured during the past centuries has made it very difficult for any profitable business or industry to develop. In the 1500s the slave trade stole human resources. Afterward, King Leopold II made a great deal of money from Congo's ivory and rubber. Belgium, too, took resources out of the country, though it also did help to grow the economy. Then the thirty-two-year reign of Mobutu Sese Seko, which ended in 1997, further sent the country into economic hardship. Mobutu plundered Congo's riches. He and his family and friends became very wealthy, while his countrymen suffered. Today neighboring countries are at war with Congo. They take mineral wealth out of the country and profit from it.

Even when people try to start businesses and create jobs, the country's lack of good roads make it hard for any enterprise to do well. It is difficult to get products to market or to ports. Fruits and vegetables spoil before they can be sold. The total length of Congo's national road system is just less then 100,000 miles (160,900 km). In the United States, which is roughly four times the size of Congo, there are more than forty times as many road miles.

Poor road conditions hamper the transport of goods and services in the Congo.

Congo's most important transportation system is the country's approximately 7,200 miles (11,600 km) of inland waterways that are navigable, meaning that boats can travel on them. This is mostly portions of the Congo River and its tributaries. There, canoes and steamers move people and products. Where the Congo is not navigable—in the regions where there are waterfalls and dangerous rapids—trains and trucks must move the goods. It is dangerous to travel even on the navigable areas today, due to all the fighting. Traffic on the river has lessened considerably.

Commercial boats depart from Kinshasa's port on the Congo River.

This sattelite dish is used to provide cellular telephone service, Internet service, and other telecom services to a slow, but growing sector of the country.

The country also has to make do with little or no piped water and electricity, especially in rural areas. Communication is challenging, since only one in every 1,250 Congolese owns a telephone. In addition, many people are poorly educated, inexperienced workers, adding to the difficulty of success. The country's economy, which was never strong, is getting worse. Its gross domestic product (GDP), or the total market value of all the goods and services produced by the nation in a year, equals $120 per person. In 1990, it had been $250 per person. The economy shrank by more than 11 percent in 2000, becoming the worst in the world. Much of the country's wealth, however, is exported illegally and thus not recorded.

In Congo, programs are in place that train farmers in agriculture, fertilizers, and seeds increasing their chances for a bountiful harvest.

Agriculture

Only 3 percent of Congo's land is arable, that is, suitable for farming. Still, about two-thirds of the country's population makes their living that way. There are many people farming a small amount of land. The food grown in Congo is not enough to feed all the Congolese people. The country has to import food from other nations.

Most farmers grow crops mainly to feed their families, with maybe a little left over to sell at local markets. The most popular of these food crops are yams, which are like sweet potatoes, and cassava, a starchy root vegetable. Other common food crops include corn, rice, peanuts, sugarcane, plantain, and pulses. Plantain is a tropical fruit, much like a banana, that is a staple in many warm climates. Pulses are plants that bear pods containing edible seeds. They are similar to peas or beans, which are also called pulses. Animals such as goats, sheep, cattle, chickens, and pigs are common farm animals.

Some Congolese farmers grow crops that are used in manufacturing. These include rubber, tapped from rubber trees; cotton, for making fabric; and palm products for oil.

Mining

The minerals stored within Congo's land have enormous value, but mining currently makes up less than 10 percent of the country's income. Congo's political instability has kept mineral production down.

Diamonds are mined mainly in Kasai-Oriental Province. Most diamonds here do not have the clarity, or clear beauty, necessary to make them valuable for jewelry, but they have industrial uses. Diamonds are one of the hardest substances known, so they are used for cutting metals and other tough materials.

Most of the Congo's mining takes place in Katanga Province. In fact, the name that Mobutu gave to Katanga Province, *Shaba*, is the Swahili word for copper. The great mineral wealth there is one of the reasons Europeans were so eager to take control of that region, and it's part of the reason fighting continues today.

There the main products mined are cobalt, copper, coltan, cassiterite (tin ore), manganese, germanium, uranium, gold, limestone, and zinc. Coltan, short for columbite-tantalite, is an ore that is found in great supply in eastern Congo and is used in the manufacturing of cell phones, computers, video games, and other high-tech products. It is mined by men digging and scraping away dirt in streambeds to get to the coltan that is underground. Mining coltan, workers can earn about four times the average national wage.

More than 4,000 metric tons of cobalt is mined in the Congo.

The Congolese government controls copper and cobalt production through the state-owned Gecamines. This huge operation dominates the mining economy, but it has had many problems in recent years. Mobutu and corrupt managers have stolen from it, while others have managed it poorly. The wars and civil unrest in the country also have hurt production.

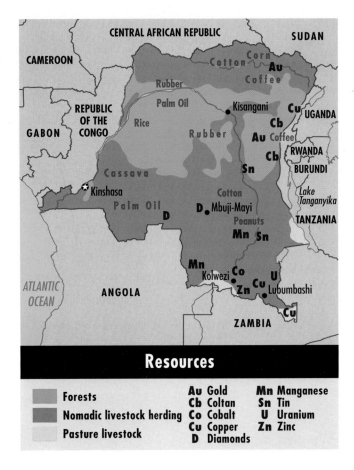

Resources

▧ Forests	**Au** Gold	**Mn** Manganese		
▧ Nomadic livestock herding	**Cb** Coltan	**Sn** Tin		
▧ Pasture livestock	**Co** Cobalt	**U** Uranium		
	Cu Copper	**Zn** Zinc		
	D Diamonds			

> Au Gold Mn Manganese
> Cb Coltan Sn Tin
> Co Cobalt U Uranium
> Cu Copper Zn Zinc
> D Diamonds

Forestry

About three-quarters of Congo's land is covered with forests, making up about 6 percent of all the world's forests. Forestry operations are another important source of income

Looting Minerals

In the 1980s Congo was one of the world's leading suppliers of industrial diamonds, but that income has declined in recent years. Neighboring countries have seized control of several of Congo's diamond mines, as well as coltan operations and other minerals.

A United Nations investigation report in 2001 stated that Uganda, Rwanda, and Burundi, and rebel soldiers from their countries, are looting Congo's resources at an incredible rate. Uganda, which has no diamond mines, has recently become one of the world's leading suppliers of diamonds. Their diamonds actually come from Congo. Additionally, the amount of gold Uganda exports is much greater than the amount it produced in recent years. Rwanda has also been exporting diamonds, coltan, and other minerals, though it produces them only in small quantities or not at all. Burundi, the UN report states, has shown similar export patterns. The income from this looting, the report concludes, has been used to continue to finance war in the region.

Congo's forests provide the country with a source of income. However, poor roads, such as the one shown above, make logging operations difficult.

for the nation, but the timber cutting there is not as extensive as it could be because of the poor infrastructure. There are few roads good enough to carry the lumber out of the forest, so most logging operations take place only in the western part of the country, near the navigable portion of the Congo River. In those areas the logs can be transported on boats down the river.

Ebony, a beautiful dark wood, is taken from Congo forests, as is teak. Teak is popular around the world for its ability to repel water, so it is often used for outdoor furniture, among other things. While these are the most valuable woods logged in Congo, other woods are harvested, too.

Manufacturing

Most of the manufacturing work in Congo is tied to mining, that is, processing of the minerals that are taken from the earth. Additional work is in processing some of the crops that are grown. Tires, shoes, fabrics, and cigarettes are also manufactured in Congo.

Hope for the Future

There is some reason to expect that Congo's economy may begin to improve. A number of economic reforms were begun in 2001 by the government, directed by Joseph Kabila. These new policies helped to greatly bring down the country's rate of

What Congo Grows, Makes, and Mines

Agriculture (1998 est.)

Coffee	21,172,000 metric tons
Palm oil	16,883,000 metric tons
Rubber	3,216,000 metric tons

Manufacturing (2000 est.)

Crushed stone	100,000 metric tons
Cement	96,000 metric tons
Limestone	25,000 metric tons

Mining (2000 est.)

Copper	21,000 metric tons
Cobalt	4,320 metric tons
Coltan	450 metric tons

inflation, or rate at which the prices of goods and services go up each year. In 2000 the inflation rate was over 500 percent, and by the end of 2002, the rate was down to 16 percent.

The country also created new mining and investment codes. Those are laws that promise fair treatment by private business owners. They should attract foreign investors. In 2002 the World Bank and the International Monetary Fund approved new credit for Congo. Investments from countries and organizations are increasing.

There is no real hope for a great improvement in Congo's economy, however, until the fighting ends. With so many groups at war for so many varied reasons, it will likely take years to calm the troubles. When that happens, finally, Congo may be able to attract more foreign investors and to build roads and factories, increase agriculture and mining, and to enhance the quality of life for its citizens.

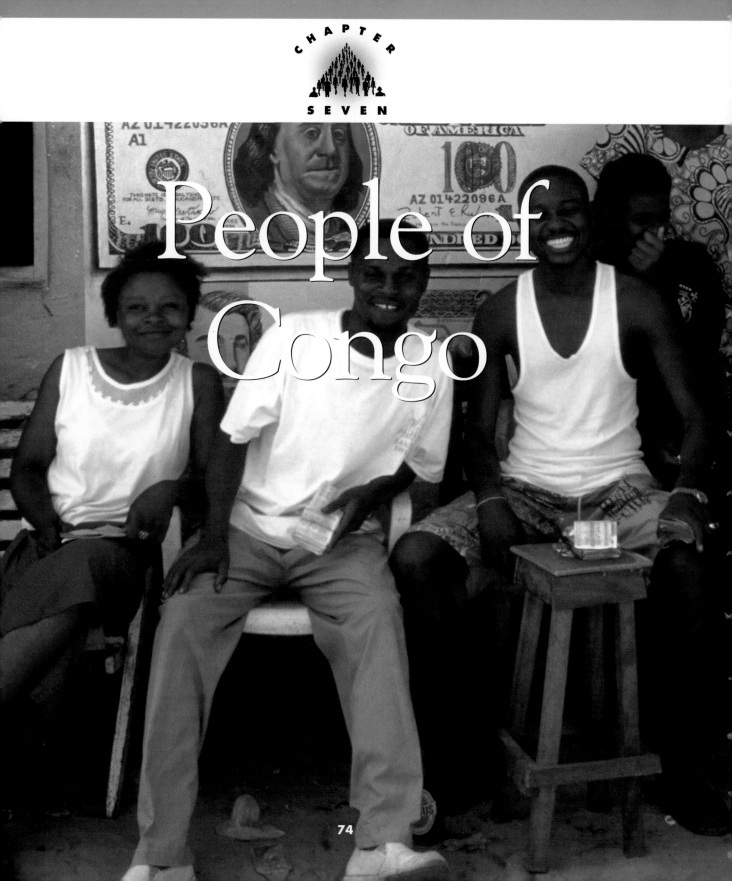

People of Congo

ORE THAN 55 MILLION PEOPLE LIVE IN CONGO. MOST live along the Congo River and its tributaries, and in the eastern highlands. The country's population is growing about 3 percent each year. For every 1,000 people in Congo, 46 babies are born and 15 people die each year. The average woman gives birth to six or seven children during her lifetime. But more than 10 percent of babies die shortly after they are born. Men can expect to live until nearly age 47; women, to 51. Almost half the population is under age 15. Only 3 percent of the people are older than 65.

Opposite: **The people of Congo have suffered through colonial rule and political conflicts. However, they have worked hard for democracy and peace.**

A Move to the City

The first people to live in Congo were rural. Today, 70 percent of the population still lives in rural areas where they can farm. But more people are moving to cities each year. This shift toward cities, or urban areas, is called urbanization.

Health care professionals are in short supply in Congo. The World Health Organization has recruited doctors to work in Congo and train local Congolese in health care practices.

People are attracted by the large number of resources and services that are only available in cities. Medical, dental, and legal assistance, for example, barely exist in rural areas. Clean, safe drinking water is available for 89 percent of the people living in cities, but only 26 percent of rural people

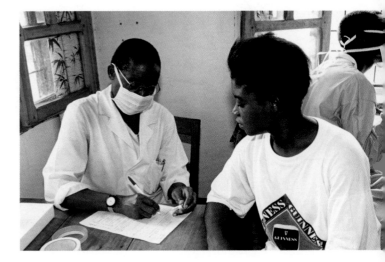

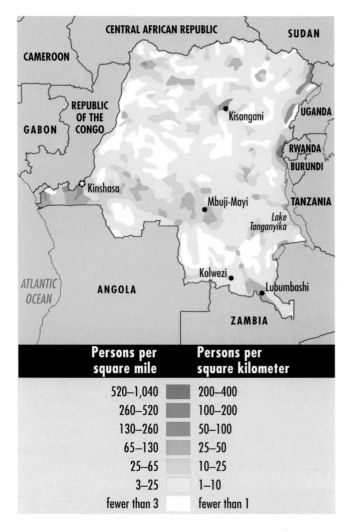

Persons per square mile	Persons per square kilometer
520–1,040	200–400
260–520	100–200
130–260	50–100
65–130	25–50
25–65	10–25
3–25	1–10
fewer than 3	fewer than 1

have access to safe water. A city also offers the hope of employment. Jobs are few, but opportunities in the city are better. The government controls food prices to make sure it is cheap enough for city dwellers to afford. But this means that rural farmers are paid poorly for the food they produce. The ethnic violence in Congo is worse in rural areas, too. Life in the city at least gives people a better chance to escape bloodshed.

Ethnic Groups

Most Congolese are black Africans, descended from people who moved into the area from other parts of Africa 2,000 years ago. Today they make up the country's more than 200 native ethnic groups. These ethnic groups are organized into larger groups based upon similarities in the languages they speak. Most people, about 80 percent, are members of Bantu-speaking groups.

The largest of Congo's ethnic groups are the Mongo, Luba, and Kongo, all of which are Bantu speaking, and the Mangbetu-Azande ethnic group, which speaks a Hamitic (a non-Semitic language such as Berber or Egyptian) language. These four groups make up 45 percent of Congo's population.

More than 40 percent of Congo's population are between the ages of 0 and 14.

Nearly all of the people of Congo are natives. Only a small number are of European descent.

The Mongo People

The Mongo people, sometimes known as the Lomongo, live mainly in the Congo Basin in the heart of Congo. This ethnic cluster is made up of several smaller, related groups. Their ancestors began arriving in the Congo Basin around A.D. 200. They pushed out the people who had inhabited the area, people who had survived by hunting and gathering, seeking out the food they needed. The Mongo also began by hunting

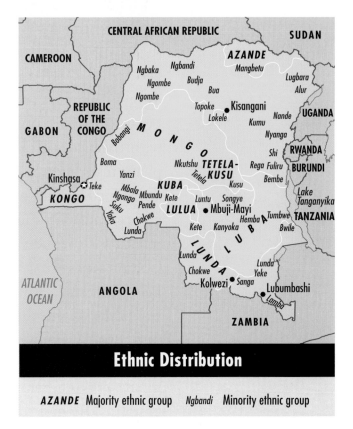

Ethnic Distribution

AZANDE Majority ethnic group   *Ngbandi*   Minority ethnic group and fishing, as well as growing such foods as yams. Through the years, they learned to cultivate more things and became great banana growers. They also became skilled at trapping animals for food and for their skins.

They were able to provide food for themselves fairly easily, and this gave them time to spend on leisure activities, such as arts and crafts. They became experts in iron working, basket weaving, and making wonderful pottery. They also constructed dugout canoes, fashioned from tree trunks, which were useful in traveling the many water systems of the Congo Basin. Surrounded by plentiful natural resources, the Mongo became wealthy through trading. They traded with neighboring people such crops as cassava, corn, and tobacco, as well as their baskets, pottery, and canoes. In return, they received such things as brass and copperware. In the mid-1800s, when Europeans began to enter Congo in search of goods, the Mongo traded with them, too. Europeans especially wanted ivory from elephant tusks and gave the Mongo European products in return.

Mongo leaders, who controlled the trade with other ethnic groups and with Europeans, were able to keep much of the wealth for themselves. Many leaders built up great fortunes. Colonialism changed all that, though. When Belgium's King Leopold II took control of the land in 1885, he also took control of the wealth that had been collected. The Mongo people were terribly exploited, as the king did anything necessary to supply the fairly new demand for rubber. Those Belgian assistants, working for the king, abused the local people and brutalized them if they tried to defend themselves.

Finally, in 1908, outside people became aware of the harsh conditions in which the Mongo people lived. There was enough outcry around the world to change the conditions somewhat, but the people still were controlled tightly by the government. They finally regained most of their freedom when the country became independent in 1960.

Today many still live in traditional ways. Their society is formed of large household groups of about twenty to forty extended family members. The senior male, known as the *tata*, or father, is the leader. Several households together form a village, led by a chief, or *bokulaka*, assisted by a council of elders. Men have high status and power in the Mongo culture, and generally hold all the leadership positions, both in society and in families.

Because they live in or near the rain forest, they are able to hunt for and gather many of the things they need, such as fish, snails, insects, mushrooms, fruits, and other foods. They also grow some foods, like bananas and cassava. They continue to produce food for sale and trade, much as they did hundreds of years ago. The Mongo people are adept at growing rubber, cotton, sugar, cocoa, and coffee for a profit.

Their language is called Mongo, or Lomongo, and they have a colorful tradition of sharing history, education, and wisdom through the stories they tell and the songs they sing.

The Luba People

People, including the Luba, have lived in Congo's Katanga region since at least A.D. 700. The system of having chiefs as the heads of tribal governments began in the north Katanga region around that time. The group of people controlled by a chief was called a chieftanship, and by the 1300s there were several strong chieftanships in the area. Conflicts arose as they fought over land, and the chieftanships began warring. It became obvious that the strongest group in the region was the Luba.

During the next two centuries, Luba society changed and developed. It established a strong central government led by a *mulopwe*, or king. People believed that the mulopwe had supernatural powers, and so they also looked up to him as a

The Luba people established a strong society that was led by a king. This is Kanonge Niembo (second from the left), a past Luba leader.

religious leader. He was assisted by the *balopwe*, a group of men selected to assist him. A *sungo* acted as a liaison between the balopwe and the people of the kingdom. There was also a man in charge of the military and the police, another was the mulopwe's religious guide, and another whose role was to step in for the mulopwe if he became sick or died.

The strong government of the Luba people made it difficult for any other group in the region to take it over. The Luba remained stable for centuries, until the late nineteenth century when East African traders, followed by King Leopold's agents, penetrated the area. The Luba suffered a terrible fate, much as the Mongo did. Today many Luba people continue to practice their traditions as much as possible. Villages, some with hundreds or even thousands of citizens, are formed by groups of families.

The people speak the language called Luba and follow the Luba religion. They make their living as hunters and slash-and-burn farmers, growing corn, cassava, mangoes, bananas, and cereal crops. Many are skilled craftsmen, turning out beautiful pottery and woodworking and blacksmithing products. Each village is led by a chief who is given some power by the government to control his village as he wishes. The Luba who have moved to large cities, however, must follow the laws of the national government.

Luba artwork is considered to be the finest in all Africa. Luba artisans held high status in society. Below is a Luba mask.

The Kongo people living in Congo today are descendants of the Kongo Kingdom, founded by a ruler named Nimi a Lukemi. This kingdom developed around A.D. 1300, near where the Congo River reaches the Atlantic Ocean. It was the largest kingdom in central Africa. It was well-organized and strong. The Kongo people were led by a king, called a *mani*. Though he was assisted by regional governors and a group of ministers, the mani had final power for ruling the people and their religious lives, as well as commanding them in warfare.

The king of Kongo receives European soldiers and their commander while seated on his throne.

Their history is quite different from that of the Mongo and Luba people. The Kongo Kingdom had ties with Portugal ever since Portuguese explorers arrived in 1482. Portugal offered military support and advice to the kingdom in return for trading rights. The kingdom sent diplomats to Europe and Brazil, and became known throughout the world.

Portugal helped the kingdom establish contact with Catholic leaders at the Vatican in Rome, Italy, which sent missionaries to the area. Most Kongo people converted to the Catholic religion, and even today the majority of them are Catholic.

The alliance with Portugal started to fall apart in the late 1500s. Groups of Kongo people began to fight among themselves over Portugal's demand for slaves. Some Kongo sought help from the Dutch, which caused a battle with the Portuguese. Finally, the Kongo kingdom split apart. Those who lived in what is now Congo became part of King Leopold's colony.

Today, many Kongo people are urban and well-educated. Most speak French in addition to their Kongo language, and work in such fields as finance, construction, and engineering. Many work in mines.

Some Kongo people still live in rural areas, usually in small villages of only a few hundred citizens. They farm, growing mainly cassava, as well as peas, rice, peppers, beans, and corn. Few raise animals for food; instead, they rely on hunting and fishing for their meat.

A Congolese family outside their hut in rural Congo.

Kongo people try to hold on to some of the traditions of their society, but it is harder for people living in cities to do this. They need to follow the rules and leadership of the national government. In rural areas, however, there still are chiefs in most villages, though they have only a limited ability to rule on their own.

An Azande witch doctor in ceremonial dress. He dances to exhaustion to put himself in touch with the spirit world.

The Azande People

The Azande people live mainly in the northern part of Congo. They formed as a group nearly 300 years ago, when the Ambomou people, led by the Avongara clan, conquered several neighboring groups. Eventually all the groups merged and became known as Azande.

They speak a variety of languages, because most still speak the language of their ancestors. Though there are differences, all these languages are considered dialects of the Azande language, which is what binds the people together as a group. There are similarities, too. Azande language is one of the African languages in which a plural changes a word at the beginning, rather than at the end. North Americans, for example, change most plurals at the end, simply by adding an "s." A good example of the Azande method is its own name. The word Azande is the plural of Zande, which would be one person.

Within Azande society there is a royal clan, from which the king is chosen. Other people are also grouped into clans based on common ancestors. These small clans are usually located around their farms, and the groups are scattered over the land. There is not much contact between the clans.

Since the Azande people were situated in the northern part of Congo, they were less affected by the terrible abuses heaped on most others by King Leopold. He basically left the area alone. But the Azande as a group were affected later when Congo and its neighboring countries gained their independence. Borders of the countries were drawn right through Azande homeland, splitting them up. Government leaders tried to force them away from their homes, which were usually along rivers, and into communities that fitted more neatly into their new boundaries. The Azande people could no longer make their living through farming and hunting as they had for centuries. They have had to learn to grow cash crops such as cotton, as the government demanded.

Congo's Great Diversity

The human diversity in Congo, with its 200 ethnic groups, is indeed great. In times past there were many obvious differences among the groups, as each had its own traditions and forms of government and religion. But in the past twenty years or so the lines between the ethnic groups have blurred. Their

Population of Major Cities

City	Population
Kinshasa	6,050,000
Lubumbashi	851,381
Mbuji-Mayi	806,475
Kolwezi	417,810
Kisangani	417,517

Poverty afflicts many in Congo. This man sorts through rubbish to find containers that he can sell at the market.

differences do not seem so obvious anymore. Each group blends in, creating a more modern society under the rule of one national government. In fact, most Congolese don't think of themselves as members of any ethnic group. Rather, their strongest bonds are with their villages, their clans, or their families.

In Congo today the greatest diversity is among economic groups. There is a small number of very wealthy people, the elite class, most of whom have some high government connections. They live in nice homes in a city, receive good educations and medical care, and enjoy most of the same luxuries as the rest of the modern world.

Next there is a slightly larger group of workers and civil servants, people who provide most of the paid labor in the country. They manage to make a meager living for themselves and their families, but the small incomes they earn are heavily taxed, and much of the tax money goes to support the elite.

At the bottom of the economic ladder is a large group of peasants. These people do not have jobs that pay regular wages. Instead, they get by in whatever way they can. In rural areas they may be hunters and gatherers, hoping to find the resources they need in nature. In some places villagers have grouped together forming co-ops. They produce crafted items or grow food crops, and sell them to raise money. More live by bartering—

trading goods or services for the things they need. For example, a small farmer may offer some of his vegetables to a doctor in return for medical treatment for his family.

The huge gap between the wealthy elite, who live in luxury, and the peasants, who struggle to get by each day, is the source of Congo's greatest diversity today.

Rwandan refugees crowd a roadway on their way from danger seeking refuge in Congo.

Refugees

In addition to the citizens of Congo, others live there as refugees. Refugees are people who have moved in from neighboring countries to escape danger in their homes. It is hard to state an exact number of refugees in the country because they are usually on the move. Some shift from one refugee camp to another and others decide to return home. Many more are killed.

Why Do People Become Refugees?

There are many reasons why people become refugees. Some leave their homes fearing that, otherwise, they will be killed because of their political beliefs. Others want to be free to practice their own religions. Sometimes, they are in fear because their ethnic background makes them a target for others filled with hatred. Wars and fighting cause people to move about in search of safer homes for their families. Droughts, floods, and other natural disasters force people out of their homes and countries as well.

People of Congo **87**

In Congo and its neighboring countries, the number of refugees is much higher than it is in most other parts of the world. Harsh conditions are fairly common there, giving people many reasons to become refugees. But the countries of this region are also quite generous in their efforts to assist refugees, establishing camps and trying to feed them, even though there isn't a lot of money to go around. The countries are usually assisted in these efforts by such international organizations as the United Nations World Food Program.

Language

The official language of Congo, used in business and government, is French. This has its direct links to the colonial era, when it was spoken by King Leopold II and the Belgians who controlled the country. But there are many other languages spoken there. Nearly every ethnic group has its own dialect. Approximately 80 percent of these are versions of Bantu. The African languages spoken most frequently are Lingala, in regions along the Congo River; Tshiluba in the south, Kikongo near the coast, and Kiswahili in the east. All four of these have also been used in official documents at times and are often heard on radio and television programs.

Most indigenous languages are spoken only, they are not written down. Ethnic groups had a strong tradition of sharing history and other information through storytelling instead. Early missionaries tried to turn some of the spoken languages into writing. In part, this was so that they could more easily learn and share the language with other missionaries, to further promote their religion. They had mixed success. Some languages are just easier to write down than others. Tshiluba was one of those that transferred better to writing, and it became one of the most common languages in Congo today.

Kikongo was the language picked up by many of the Europeans who came to Congo in the 1800s. They first learned it from ethnic groups near the coast where they landed. Then they helped to promote its spread eastward through the nation. Kiswahili moved through the nation in the opposite direction. It was spoken in the east, picked up by Arab slave traders who entered Congo there, and then carried westward by them.

Lingala has prospered as a language because, as the language of ethnic groups located along the Congo River, it was important for Europeans to speak it as they tried to control trade on the Congo. European military and trading people learned to speak it, and they spread it wherever they went. Additionally, much of the most popular music in Congo is sung in the Lingala language. These recorded songs are played on radio stations throughout the country, thus keeping the language alive.

With all the different languages in the country, most Congolese have learned to speak several of them. They may use French in business or when dealing with the government. When they are at home with family and friends, they may use the dialect of their ethnic group. And when they are out with others, they may speak one of the common native languages, such as Kikongo or Lingala.

Common Words and Phrases

Mbote	Hello
Nakeyi	Goodbye
Sango nini?	How are you?
Limbisa	Please
Matondo	Thank you
Eh	Yes
Te	No

Overlapping Faiths

N EARLY 50 PERCENT OF THE CONGOLESE PEOPLE ARE
Roman Catholic, another 20 percent or so are Protestant.
Maybe 10 percent follow the indigenous Kimbanguist Church,
10 percent are Muslim, and the remaining Congolese, about 10
percent, follow various traditional African religions.

Those are not very specific statistics, but specifics are not possible when there is so much overlapping of religions. Very few people in Congo follow one religious group exclusively. Catholics, for example, may carry figurines from their native religions while performing a difficult task, such as taking a test, to give them power and wisdom. A Protestant may use a traditional magic chant to help a loved one who is sick. A follower of a traditional religion may go to a Christian missionary for help with a particular spiritual need. Most Congolese are willing to seek whichever spiritual assistance seems to be most useful in any given situation.

Opposite: **A pastor stands at the alter at an Assembly of God church in Bukavu.**

Religions of Congo

Roman Catholic	50%
Protestant faiths	20%
Kimbanguist	10%
Other traditional African religions	10%
Muslim	10%

These percentages are not exact, for there is a good deal of overlapping of religions among the population.

Roman Catholics of Congo

Roman Catholicism is the largest religious faith in Congo. It was introduced by Portuguese missionaries in the late 1400s, during the time when the Kongo people had strong ties with Portugal. They believe in one God, the creator of all the universe.

The Catholic Church has played a very important role in Congo. Not only does it claim more followers than any other religion, but primary responsibility for many important services in the country have fallen to it. Catholic schools educate about half of the country's children. Hospitals and clinics run by the Catholic Church provide much of the needed medical care to the nation. The church also creates employment for many people through the farms, stores, and other businesses it sponsors.

Fifty percent of Congolese are Roman Catholic. This woman holds a papal flag and cross to welcome a visit from Pope John Paul II.

The Catholic Church provides education for many Congolese.

Congolese Catholics often blend their faith with the traditional religious beliefs of their ethnic group. Some follow the Jamaa movement, which has taken off from the Catholic Church. It was established by a Franciscan priest, Placide Tempels, in 1953. Tempels based it on Catholic teachings, along with Bantu beliefs. He organized small groups of Congolese Catholics. They meet regularly in search of an emotional encounter with God. Members of the Jamaa movement, which means "family" in Kiswahili, are still Catholics, though, officially, the Catholic church takes a dim view of it.

The Protestant Religions

The first Protestant missionaries arrived in Congo in 1878. Shortly after their arrival King Leopold II founded the Congo Free State, which we have seen brought with it many abuses against the native people. The Protestant missionaries were among the first to speak out against the terrible things they witnessed. Their complaints helped bring an end to the horrors when they created enough worldwide objection to the abuses led by King Leopold.

Today, the Protestant churches of Congo are well respected and appreciated by the people. Not only do they provide many necessary services, such as schooling and medical care, but they also monitor corruption in government and business. Protestant and Catholic churches both have been asked by government leaders to encourage members to join various government boards and agencies in order to oversee operations and to promote ethical practices.

The Religious Calendar

Approximately 70 percent of Congolese are Roman Catholics or Protestants. They follow a similar religious calendar.

Good Friday	March or April
Easter	March or April
Christmas	December 25

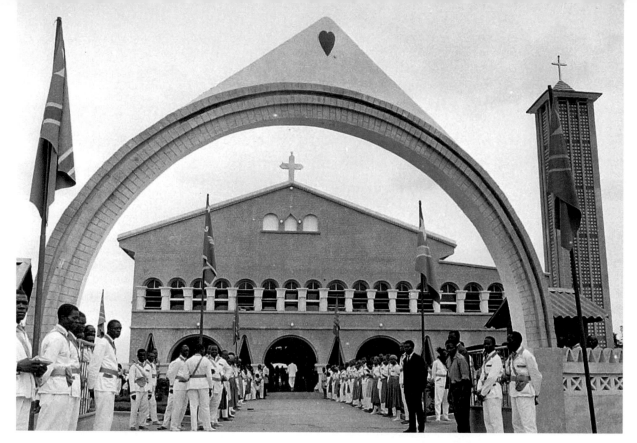

A Kimbanguist church holds a special ceremony to celebrate their anniversary.

The Kimbanguist Church

The Kimbanguist Church, also known as the Church of Jesus Christ on Earth, had its start in Congo in the early 1920s. Simon Kimbangu was a Baptist preacher in his early thirties then, touring Congo and drawing large crowds wherever he went. He kept audiences spellbound with his tales about his visions from God. Though he based his message on Protestant teachings, he added stricter rules. Followers had to get rid of all forms of their native religions, including charms, dance drums, and other sacred objects. They had to give up all belief in magic and witchcraft. Men were allowed to have only one wife. Followers had to completely obey Kimbangu and his associates. Still, his popularity spread throughout Congo. As it did, people would travel on foot for miles to beg him to cure their diseases and even to bring the dead back to life.

Kimbangu's influence spread throughout Congo, and the Belgian government authorities began to worry. They didn't want Kimbangu or anyone else to become too powerful. They didn't like it either when he spoke out against Christian missionaries and other aspects of European culture. The Belgian authorities arrested Kimbangu and put him in jail for the rest of his life.

Kimbangu's followers were the authorities' next target. The Belgians believed that if his followers were split up, their influence on others would crumble. Kimbangu's followers were arrested and sent away to places throughout the country. This plan didn't work the way the Belgians wanted it to. It actually helped strengthen the faith. Wherever they went, Kimbangu's followers preached, and now their message was heard through-out the country. Soon the religion had grown far and wide.

Kimbangu died in prison in 1951. By then, his church was strong. His son Joseph became its leader. Still, followers were forced to meet secretly, because of harassment from the government. They would gather in remote locations, hoping they would not be found and arrested. Finally the government grew tired of tracking the church and formally recognized the Kimbanguist Church in 1959. It became one of only three Christian churches formally recognized in the country, with the others being the Roman Catholic Church, and the Protestant Church of Christ.

Kimbanguists celebrate only three religious holidays: Christmas, or the birth of Christ, on December 25; April 6,

Simon Kimbangu

Simon Kimbangu was the founder of the religion named for him, the Kimbanguist Church. He was a Kongo born in 1887, the son of a leader of one of Congo's traditional religions. When he was twenty-eight, he and his wife were converted by Baptist missionaries. Kimbangu soon joined their cause, helping others prepare for baptism into Christianity. In 1918, the year in which a serious influenza epidemic brought sickness to much of the world, he had a dream in which God told him to preach and heal the sick. Kimbangu didn't want to. Instead, he moved to Leopoldville, where he worked with poor people. But at age thirty-four, he cured a sick woman and realized he had to follow his calling. He began preaching and healing, drawing large crowds.

Kimbangu believed himself to be much like Jesus Christ. As Jesus did, he appointed twelve apostles to help in his mission. People quickly agreed to his strict demands, to the surprise of many missionaries who had worked for years to get people to give up their native religions. Kimbangu was attractive to so many in Congo for he was an African, too. The Congolese often mistrusted the European missionaries, whom they felt tried to convert them but did not share the secrets that led to the same kind of material wealth the Europeans enjoyed. Kimbangu would share those secrets, many believed.

Kimbangu didn't have much time to preach. He was arrested only six months after his mission began, and spent the rest of his life in prison, where he died in 1951. His church survived and remains strong today.

when Kimbangu's ministry of healing began; and October 12, the day Kimbangu died in prison. Worship ceremonies usually last several hours, and are very joyful events. Participants pray, sing, wave palm branches, and donate money generously.

Traditional African Religions

There were many forms of traditional religions in the Congo, since nearly every ethnic group had its own. A few still exist today. Many Congolese practice the traditional religions along with their Christian faiths, while others remain true only to their native religion. Though there is a wide variety of beliefs among the traditional religions, there are a few things common to nearly all of them.

Usually there is one god that is supreme, the creator of all things. Most of the traditional African religions involve the magic and power of the spirit world. They revere dead ancestors; natural forces and elements, such as violent weather, water, and animals; as well as mythical gods.

The native religions helped the ethnic groups in many ways. First, they provided a way of explaining things in the natural world. They could credit the gods and spirits for such things as the abundance of game and wildlife or the lack of it, destructive weather, disease, and invading forces. The religions also imposed a moral code on the people, so that everyone behaved in similar and predictable ways. This made it easier for a group to stick together, to protect each other. Finally, the native religions often had sacred leaders in charge. These men were believed to have special powers and were often the heads of the community. So the religions gave social structure to the ethnic groups.

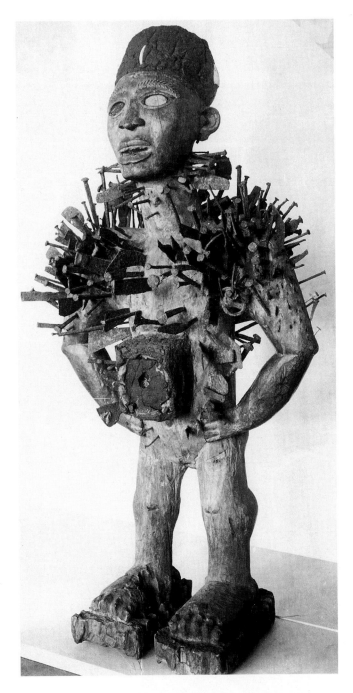

Tribespeople believe this statue wards off illnesses.

Expression Through the Arts

F OR CENTURIES, WHEN PEOPLE IN CONGO WANTED TO SHARE an idea, information, or news of an event, they used art. They sang a song, carved a statue, or told a story. These people, with no written language, used these mediums to express themselves. Even today, when there are many modern options, such as newspapers, computers, and the Internet, Congolese turn to art, music, literature, and even sports, as a way to draw people together.

Opposite: **Congolese tribeswomen perform a cultural song as a way to share and express themselves.**

Early Artwork

People have been creating objects of beauty and meaning in Congo throughout their history. Archaeologists have found evidence of animal sculptures in the region that date back to A.D. 800. Wooden masks with animal features have also been located from that time. Most of the artwork in Congo revolved around the themes of leadership, death, and the spiritual world.

A Congolese ivory animal sculpture

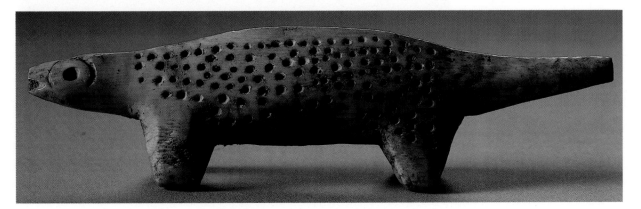

Modern Congolese paintings, such as this, are influenced by the art of the past.

Today, when artists in Congo paint, sculpt, or assemble, much of what they create is influenced by ancient art. Many of the art forms created now are similar to what was done 100 or more years ago. Artists in Congo still use their work to express their ideas and feelings about these same topics.

Art of the Kongo Kingdom

The Kongo Kingdom was the largest, wealthiest, and most powerful kingdom in central Africa during the two centuries prior to Congo's colonization. Its culture of arts flourished during this period, when skilled artists produced many beautiful works. That art was frequently used to establish the superiority of the king and his chiefs. They wore clothing made of finely woven textiles. They sat upon thrones embellished with carvings and ornamentation. They carried beautiful staffs carved of ivory and wore elaborate headgear. These fine objects often were believed to hold special powers, and they passed on these powers to the rulers who owned them.

Christianity was introduced to the Kongo people in the late 1400s by Portuguese missionaries, and soon

A royal headdress decorated with feathers, shells, and buttons

With the introduction of Christianity, religious symbols became art in Congo. This is a crucifix made of bronze.

the king made it the official Kongo religion. The new religious beliefs added another dimension to Congo art. Soon crucifixes, depicting Christ's death on the cross, were being cast in copper or carved from ivory. They were in some ways copies of the crucifixes the missionaries brought from Europe, but the Kongo artists added their own features. The representations were more abstract, and Christ appeared on many to have an African face.

Art of the Lunda Empire

Though the Lunda people are not a major part of Congo's population today, the Lunda Empire dominated the region south and east of the Kongo Kingdom during the 1500s and until the time of colonization. Lunda were skilled hunters, who used their abilities to take down large animals, including elephants, and to take control of neighboring people. The Lunda were smart and strong, yet they never developed any art forms that were strictly their own. Rather, they copied styles from the neighbors they controlled, especially the Chokwe to the west.

Chokwe tradition was rich in detailed woodcarving, and the Lunda picked this up. Chiefs, especially, were owners of very ornate stools, staffs, and statues. Typically, all of these would have abstract human figures carved into them. Carvings on the staffs often represented past chiefs, who were believed to have gone on to the spirit world and could continue to provide insight and guidance from there.

Minkisi

Minkisi are a type of sacred art that is believed to protect people from evil spirits and sickness and to ensure success in warfare. They can take many forms but are usually containers, such as hollowed-out gourds, clay pots, shells, or baskets. These vessels hold a spiritual item, often relics from the grave of an important, powerful ancestor. The strengths of these dead people are believed to pass into the minkisi and, from there, into those who own the minkisi.

The Kongo people have made minkisi for centuries and continue to make them today. But they played their most important role during the colonial period. Kongo people used them in an attempt to fend off the abuse and control heaped upon them by Belgian and other European colonists. The minkisi were often taken away by missionaries, who used them as proof of the Kongo people's ongoing belief in pagan religions.

Mukanda Masks

Masks were an important aspect of Chokwe culture, representing spirits of ancestors and the natural world. They were used in hunting and fertility rituals and during ceremonies anointing a new chief. Masks were also used during the *mukanda*, a lengthy rite of passage during which a boy becomes a man. Different forms of the mukanda were practiced by various ethnic groups throughout Congo. Spirit guides, represented by some thirty different masks, helped the boys through this process. Most masks are crafted using a mixture of cloth, resins, and wood. Mukanda masks are still made and used today, but they are mostly for entertainment. Actors wear them in plays as they show the audience scenes from life in the Congo long ago.

The Business of Art

Today, throughout the world there is a big demand for traditional African artwork. The ethnic tribal look is a popular form of decorating in many homes. Tourists in Africa like to buy it as souvenirs, and people also buy exported African art at shops and boutiques throughout North America and Europe. This provides an important source of income for artists in Africa. But it has a negative aspect, too. Most people are seeking primitive art forms, like that which was produced by artists for centuries. This keeps today's artists locked into making the same kind of art over and over, if they want to make any money for their work and support their families. They feel this demand prevents them from creating a modern style of African art, representing the twenty-first century.

Literature

Few poems, novels, or social commentaries were published in Congo until the period leading up to its independence, in 1960. Until then, colonial control, along with a lack of education in written language, prevented the growth of literature in the country. But it has been a growing trend ever since. Most works are written in local Bantu languages, although some are also written in French.

Among the country's notable authors is Clementine Faik-Nzuji, born in 1944. She has won several prizes for her short stories and poetry, and is also known for her work in studying the Bantu language, its history and symbolism. Her 1968 book of poetry, *Livres*, is one of the first written and published in French by an African female writer. Author and poet Pius Ngandu Nkashama, born in Mbuji-Mayi, has taught in universities throughout the world. He has written several novels and plays, and a 1977 book of poems was reprinted in 1997.

Music

Music is an important way for Congolese to express themselves, just as art is. Some pop-music stars are big celebrities at home. Other musicians, who specialize in traditional ethnic music, are often known only in their villages. But all have contributed in some way to the country's rich musical heritage.

Congolese ethnic music has a long history, though it's somewhat different in each group. Drums have long been used to create rhythm, and set the mood for various events. The country's earliest inhabitants were the Pygmies, and their music set the stage for all that followed. They kept the beat with sticks, drummed in short, repetitious patterns. Songs included a lot of rich vocal harmonies, and many of their songs spoke of hunting and the need for survival.

Today many villages have a small group of people who serve as village historians. They hand down stories through song, from generation to generation. They tell about events and personalities from the village's past. But many songs are about life today, revolving around daily tasks. Singing these songs helps to bring a little fun to boring jobs. They use a variety of instruments, including flutes carved from bamboo, trumpets made from gourds or animal hides, drums, and stringed instruments.

A Congolese man plays a homemade stringed instrument.

Pop Music

The country's pop music has taken the basics of ethnic music from the country's rural areas and combined it with urban, up-to-date elements. Modern instruments, electronic sounds, and foreign influences are all a part. Congolese pop music had its roots in the 1930s, when rural people moved to the cities. They learned to play guitars and heard different music on radios and record players. Many especially enjoyed mambo music from Cuba, because it has African roots and was similar to those old ethnic tunes. Pop musicians incorporated Cuban guitars and pianos into their songs. Bands featuring as many as five guitars were common. By the 1960s, when the country was in the early years of its independence, Kinshasa and other large Congolese cities each had its own musical sound, as well. Some call it rumba or soukous or Congo music. Whatever the name, it is gaining in popularity throughout all of Africa and parts of Europe.

Popular Musicians

One of the biggest celebrities in Congo's pop culture is Werrason, the lead singer from the group Wenge Maison Mère. He was born on Christmas Day, 1965, in Moalimbo, and named Ngiama Noel Makanda. It is his role not only to be a singer, he believes, but to be an educator as well. Through his music, he's said, he hopes to share the truth about life as an African man. Critics say that he lacks talent and his musical messages are clichés. But they can't dispute Werrason's popularity. His pop-African tunes sell hundreds of thousands of albums. In 2001 he was chosen as "the best central African singer," and "the best African star."

Kofi Olomide, a singer of Lingala music, also has a huge following in Congo. The Lingala music sound begins with Congo's ethnic music roots and blends in influences from all over: rumba from Cuba; saxophones, trumpets, and other band instruments from Europe; rock and roll and rap from America. It all combines in dance music that is unique to Congo and is getting more popular around the world. Kofi and Lingala music are a source of pride to young Congolese.

Congolese music is wildly popular in its homeland. When one Kinshasa band, Wenge Maison Mère, returned home from an eight-month tour of Europe and North America, it was necessary to use an army tank to carry members safely through the dancing crowds in the streets. In a country torn apart by fighting, music helps bring unity.

Sports

As it does in so many countries, soccer rules the sports world in Congo. Children play it in the streets and in schools, and many people follow professional teams.

Soccer is one of the few organized sports supported by the country. Kinshasa has a major stadium, and most schools and communities sponsor teams. There is also a national team. Soccer seems to bring a positive sense of unity to Congo. In 2002 there was great excitement over the national soccer team, which had a good chance to win the African National Cup finals. No Congolese soccer team had really done well since 1974, when Congo became the first nation from sub-Saharan Africa to have a team qualify for the World

Congo's Kituele Yuvuladio (right) fights for the ball at the 2002 African National Cup soccer tournament.

Basketball Stars

Two professional basketball players in the United States call Congo home. Mwadi Mabika (above left) was born in 1976 in Kinshasa. She grew up playing basketball on the street, and earned a spot on her country's Olympic team in 1996. Today, she is a leading scorer for the WNBA's Los Angeles Sparks. She hopes to set up a foundation to bring basketball equipment to youngsters in Congo, to give them the same opportunities to play that she's enjoyed.

Dikembe Mutombo (above right), was center for the Philadelphia 76ers, and most recently, the New York Knicks, also hails from Kinshasa. In 2001 he was named the NBA Defensive Player of the Year. He is using many of the millions he earns as a professional player to improve health care in his hometown. Mutombo is helping to finance and support a 300-bed hospital, using his own money, and working hard to raise more donations. He knows that even when the building is complete, it will cost millions more each year to keep the hospital in operation, and he wants to provide it. Mutombo was moved to start the hospital following the death of his mother. She died in Kinshasa because she couldn't get proper medical care. He hopes that fewer people will have to die from such diseases as malaria, cholera, and polio.

Cup. Though the 2002 Congolese team was eliminated in the quarterfinals by Senegal, it brought a lot of excitement to the nation, which greatly needed the lift.

But Congolese enjoy many other sports, too. Basketball is growing in popularity. A number of young people participate in track and field events, while others enjoy volleyball and boxing.

"We may be divided," said Congolese sports reporter Ngoyi Kapuka, "but sports and music keep the Congolese people together."

Marriage Customs of the Congo

Marriages are steeped in cultural customs in Congo. Though marriages used to be commonly arranged by the parents, today this is unusual, especially in urban areas. Young men and women typically choose their own partners. In those areas where marriages are arranged, the man often pays money, called a bride-price, to the woman's parents. If the couple gets divorced, the man will sometimes get back the bride-price.

Many couples have both a civil ceremony and a religious ceremony, with the celebrations—food, music, dancing, and gift-giving—going on for days. Among some Bantu ethnic groups the bride wears a *kitenge*, which is a colorful, flowing gown. The *duluga*, a dance with many elaborate steps, is performed during the ceremony.

Because there are so many ethnic backgrounds, each with its own traditions, it is impossible to pinpoint specific customs common to all Congolese. But in all traditions, marriage is a big event. As time goes on and the couple welcomes children into the marriage,

there is more celebration. Children are prized in Congo, and big families are common.

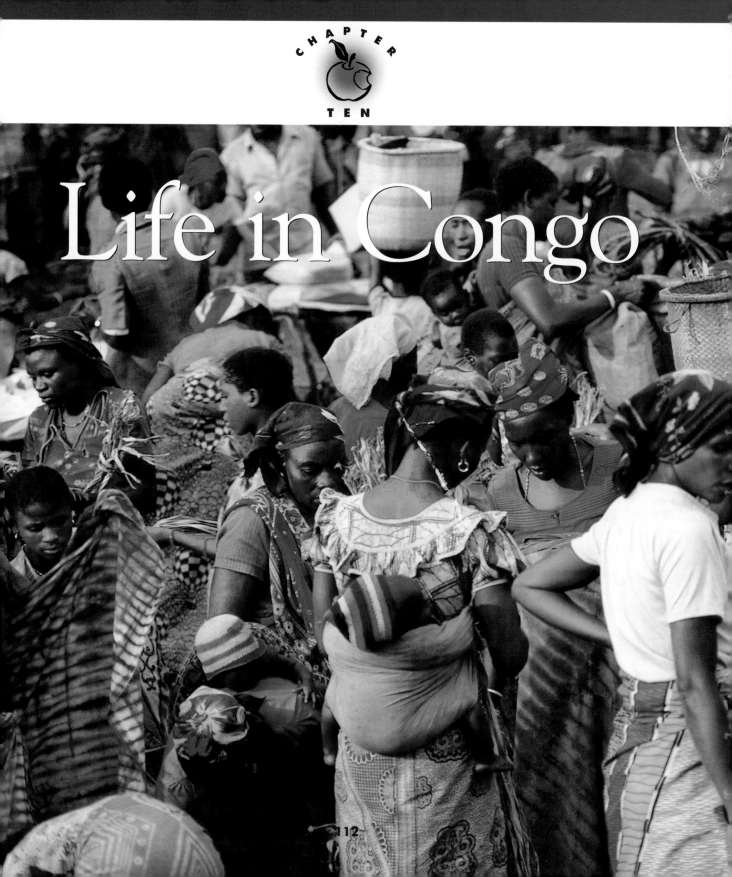

Life in Congo

Rural life in Congo centers on farming. Here, a woman harvests potatoes.

THERE IS NOT JUST ONE SORT OF WAY TO LIVE IN CONGO. Customs, traditions, and opportunities vary greatly. Some people living in large cities have very modern lives, similar to people in the United States and Canada. They shop in large stores, drive cars, watch television, use the Internet. Other people, living in remote villages, have lives that are much like those of their ancestors from 100 years ago. If they want food, clothing, or shelter, they go into the forest and find materials for it. They walk or use dugout canoes to get around. They share information by word of mouth and may not wear much clothing at all. Some people live in refugee camps or hide in the forest to escape fighting. For them, simply staying alive is a daily struggle.

There are, indeed, many ways to live in Congo. Farming in rural areas of the country, however, is the most common. Most farmers are poor. Even though the land is rich and productive,

Opposite: **Life in Congo is diverse and depends on the customs and traditions of each group.**

Cassava

Cassava is the mainstay of the Congo diet. It's grown by nearly all people living in rural areas throughout the country. Little of the plant goes to waste. The leaves are eaten as greens, usually boiled. The roots are dried and ground into a flour, called manioc meal. This flour is then mixed into fou-fou, a kind of dough.

farmers don't have the tools necessary to grow large amounts of food. Even if they did, not enough transportation is available to deliver and sell it to people in more urban areas of the country. So they grow only enough to feed themselves and their families.

Food

Cassava, corn, and rice are staples of the Congo diet. These are the starchy foods that most people live on and eat every

Vegetables are an ingredient in many Congolese dishes.

day. Farmers can grow them fairly easily throughout the country, and they can be dried and stored for eating during months when they don't grow.

Most people eat two meals a day, at noon and in the early evening. Meals are usually a starchy stew, served with vegetables and spices. If an animal or fish has been caught, these might be added to the mix. Poultry is available, but dried and smoked fish are eaten more often. Still, this

Moambé

This is a chicken dish popular throughout Congo.

Ingredients:

3 lbs. chicken, cut into pieces

2 onions, chopped

2 Tbs. curry

1 tsp. paprika

$\frac{1}{2}$ tsp. ginger

2 large potatoes, peeled and diced

6 oz. tomato paste

4 Tbs. creamy peanut butter

1 tsp. hot pepper

1 cup water

12 oz. fresh mushrooms, diced

1 box frozen chopped spinach

Sauté chicken and onion until chicken in browned and onion is transparent; add curry, paprika, ginger, potatoes, tomato paste, peanut butter, hot pepper, and water. Add salt. Add mushrooms and spinach; simmer 10 minutes or until chicken is done. Serve hot over steamed rice.

A Change in Culture

Mobutu Sese Seko definitely had a great impact on the politics and history of his country, but he also made an impact on its eating preferences. At the time that he took power, foods served in the country's fine restaurants had a strong Belgian influence. Steaks, heavy sauces, sweet pastries, and other European-type delicacies were popular. But Mobutu ordered the country to become more authentically African. Restaurant cuisine was forever changed. Traditional African dishes became far more popular, and today such foods as goat, river catfish, and thick, spicy stews with chicken or beef are common on menus.

is not an everyday meal. Most Congolese don't eat much meat and lack enough protein in their diets. Malnutrition is, unfortunately, quite common. Meat is usually eaten just for special occasions.

Building a Rural Home

Techniques used in building the mud homes so common throughout Congo differ depending upon where the home is located, because of different soil types. In Katanga Province, for example, in the southern part of the country, the soil has a heavy clay content. But in Bandundu, in the west central part of Congo, there's mostly sandy soil.

A strong frame is needed to keep such sandy soils in place, so in Bandundu, home builders securely tie together sticks and palm fronds to begin the house. They use rope made from a vine found in nearby marshes. They add more fronds to this frame to create a roof. Then the entire structure is covered in a paste made of the sandy soil mixed with water. If the homeowner can afford a little cement, this is sometimes added, too, to make it stronger. Then a thatch roof made of grass is placed on top of the structure to carry the rain away from the building. Usually, thatch roofs will last about two years before termites ruin them. Then they are replaced with new thatch bundles.

In Katanga the clay soils make it easy to build brick houses. The best clay is often found in termite mounds, since the termites carry up the richest clay soil, which is found beneath the surface. Moist clay is mixed with straw, pressed into brick molds, then set in the sun to dry. Next, the bricks are baked in a homemade brick oven, where the heat from a fire burning inside will make them even stronger. Once cooled, the bricks are ready for building. Cement is sometimes used for mortar to hold the bricks together, but it is often hard to get. Builders usually use a chalk mixture that they can get locally.

Walls of dried mud and roofs of sticks make up a rural Congolese home.

Housing

In rural areas the most common housing is made of dried mud, sometimes mixed with sticks. A few homes have metal roofs. These usually belong to wealthier families. The owners can collect the rainwater that runs off them, and use it for washing and for feeding animals. It means fewer trips to the river or pump to haul water home. Most homes, though, have thatched roofs, made with large bundles of grass tied together and attached to the roof.

This family lives in an apartment found in urban Congo.

Large cinder block apartment buildings are home to many people living in Congo's bigger cities. Those who work at jobs in offices and factories can usually afford such homes. Some of the nation's wealthiest people, such as those who run businesses and the government, live in pretty single-family homes with nice yards. But poor people living in cities often crowd into areas filled with cheap homes made of mud bricks. Here, there are few of the services that wealthy people enjoy, such as access to fresh water and garbage collection.

Clothing

In Congo's farming villages, most people wear very casual clothing. The men wear loose cotton shirts and shorts, while the women wear flowing skirts and blouses or dresses. Some of the remote tribes wear little clothing at all, or fashion some of large leaves.

Women in rural Congo wear long dresses of colorful fabric.

People who live in the city usually wear more formal clothes. Women wear clothing similar to that worn in the warmer climates of North America. Men wear a suit of slacks with a matching jacket. The jacket usually has no collar and is worn without a shirt or tie.

On the chalkboard:
l u o a l u o a
l'école de rémi   une flèche
é   é   è
bébé   élève épi vélo
le papa de rémi est grand
rémi est petit
il a un beau petit vélo
le petit vélo de rémi
maman a un beau bébé

Education is valued in Congo. Some children travel far each day to schools that are in poor condition.

Education

Though Congo's laws say that every child in the nation shall attend school from the age of six through twelve, this isn't strictly enforced. Enforced schooling really isn't practical in many rural areas. There simply isn't enough money for teachers and supplies to take to schools in some of the remote places in Congo. About two-thirds of all school-age male children go to elementary school, and about half of all Congolese girls attend.

A good education in Congo is highly prized. The government spends more money on education than it does on most other areas of government. Parents see schooling as the one thing that can somehow help their children get out of poverty. Many people go to great lengths to get an education for their children. Some will travel great distances each day to get to school.

In some small villages, they make major sacrifices in order to provide a basic education, setting up little schools. Unfortunately, these schools are not always well equipped or well run, and the students don't learn all they should. Congo has a nationwide test every child must pass in order to get a diploma, and many students from the small rural schools fail the test.

Those students who do pass the test have the opportunity to attend high school in a large city if they wish, and this is

College students studying labor laws at a university in Kinshasa.

becoming more common. Beyond high school, the nation does have some universities, including two in the capital of Kinshasa, as well as in Kisangani, Lubumbashi, and Bukavu.

Holidays

Religious holidays are festive times in Congo, and people celebrate as grandly as they are able. If a family can afford to roast a cow or a goat, they probably will. Most are not wealthy enough, but will do as much as they can to enjoy the holiday and honor their religion. Since most Congolese are Christian, the main religious holidays observed are Christmas and Easter.

Holidays in Congo	
New Year's Day	January 1
Easter	March or April
Labor Day	May 1
Independence Day	June 30
Parents' Day	August 1
Christmas	December 25

There are a few other holidays, mostly because there is so much poverty and unrest in the country. It is hard for people to get the peaceful free time and money needed to really enjoy holidays. New Years Day is observed, and so is Independence Day. A popular holiday unique to Congo is Parents' Day, held each year on August 1. On this day, people honor their dead ancestors in the morning and celebrate their living families in the afternoon. They begin by going to the cemetery to clean the graves of their deceased family members. Any overgrown brush and tall grasses are burned down. Then they sweep around the graves and wipe down the headstones. Many families share a picnic lunch at the cemetery when their work is done. The rest of the day is spent at home, with parents and children relaxing together, enjoying good food and playing games.

A rural health care giver works from her office.

Health Care

Health care has improved in Congo since 1960, when the country became independent. At that time, nearly all the country's doctors were Europeans, and they usually left. The few Congolese nurses and technicians who remained took care of most of the population, assisted by missionaries. The government quickly established medical training programs, and today there is one doctor for every 14,000 people or so. This is better than it was, but still poor by the standards of the United States and Canada. The country's political problems and fighting, along with a lack of government funding, are again causing a serious decline in the level of health care in Congo. The very wealthy and the very sick get most of the medical attention. Pregnant women, though, can go to special centers set up in most cities to provide care for them and their newborns.

Most of this medical care is available in the cities. Businesses and factories are required by law to provide medical care for their employees. Rural farmers, though, don't get that protection. It is difficult for people in remote regions to get treatment unless they travel long distances. There are, however, a few hospital boats that travel the Congo River. Those are staffed with medical professionals and equipped with supplies to treat some needs of those living along the river. Various epidemics, however, are putting strains on the limited medical resources available. In the last decade, the Congo has seen an increase in such diseases as cholera, malaria, measles, and HIV/AIDS.

The government is working to help get rid of serious diseases that still kill many Congolese. It has joined with the World Health Organization and other medical agencies to try to put an end to leprosy, tuberculosis, polio, and sleeping sickness.

Ding-Dingo

The Kongo people play a traditional game called ding-dingo. Players jump through a maze laid out with stones on the ground. They keep track of how well they do by using counters. This game requires a great deal of skill. People who are good at it appear almost to be dancing as they make their way through the maze. Ding-dingo is not simply a game for enjoyment. Kongo people believe that it also has a deeper meaning, representing the mystical world that follows life here on earth.

Recreation

In their free time nearly all Congolese enjoy getting together with friends, family, and neighbors for dancing, music, talking, and food and drinks. Those kinds of social events are enjoyed in rural areas and in cities. There are many other opportunities in cities, of course, such as concerts and sporting events.

Congolese enjoy having a good time. A nightclub in Kisangani is the place to dance and relax with friends.

For many who live in Congo, time for recreation is only a dream. Those living amid poverty and war must struggle every moment to survive. The nation and its neighbors must strive to work out their differences so that someday every child born will have a chance to simply enjoy a nice meal, get an education, and play a game among friends.

The Congolese hope for a future of peace for their children.

Life in Congo   **127**

Timeline

Congolese History		World History	
Pygmies moved into Congo region.	**Unknown**		
		2500 B.C.	Egyptians build the Pyramids and the Sphinx in Giza.
		563 B.C.	The Buddha is born in India.
Bantu-speaking people join Pygmies.	**A.D. 1**		
People of Congo region establish complex kingdoms.	**1–1500**	A.D. 313	The Roman emperor Constantine recognizes Christianity.
		610	The Prophet Muhammad begins preaching a new religion called Islam.
		1054	The Eastern (Orthodox) and Western (Roman) Churches break apart.
		1066	William the Conqueror defeats the English in the Battle of Hastings.
		1095	Pope Urban II proclaims the First Crusade.
		1215	King John seals the Magna Carta.
Kongo Kingdom is established.	**1300s**	1300s	The Renaissance begins in Italy.
		1347	The Black Death sweeps through Europe.
		1453	Ottoman Turks capture Constantinople, conquering the Byzantine Empire.
Portuguese navigators arrive.	**1482**	1492	Columbus arrives in North America.
Portuguese begin slave trading, assisted by Kongo people.	**1500s**	1500s	The Reformation leads to the birth of Protestantism.
Other Europeans and Arabs are slave trading.	**1700s**	1776	The Declaration of Independence is signed.
		1789	The French Revolution begins.
		1865	The American Civil War ends.
Henry Morton Stanley makes first Congo exploration; meets David Livingstone.	**1871**		
Stanley makes second Congo exploration.	**1874–1877**		

Congolese History

Stanley makes third visit to Congo, sponsored by King Leopold II of Belgium.	1879–1884
King Leopold establishes the Congo Free State.	1885
Belgian Parliament annexes Congo, creating the Belgian Congo.	1908
Congolese troops fight in World War I with Allied troops.	1914–1918
Alliance of Kongo People calls for immediate independence.	1956
Belgian Congo is granted independence. Becomes the Republic of Congo.	1960
Joseph-Désiré Mobutu takes control of country following a coup.	1965
Mobutu changes country name to Zaire and own name to Mobutu Sese Seko.	1971
Mobutu forced out of office. Laurent Kabila assumes presidency. Country is named Democratic Republic of the Congo.	1997
Kabila is assassinated. His son, Joseph Kabila, becomes president.	2001
Negotiations over the withdrawal of foreign troops and on a reconciliation among all Congolese factions.	2002

World History

1914	World War I breaks out.
1917	The Bolshevik Revolution brings communism to Russia.
1929	Worldwide economic depression begins.
1939	World War II begins, following the German invasion of Poland.
1945	World War II ends.
1957	The Vietnam War starts.
1969	Humans land on the moon.
1975	The Vietnam War ends.
1979	Soviet Union invades Afghanistan.
1983	Drought and famine in Africa.
1989	The Berlin Wall is torn down, as communism crumbles in Eastern Europe.
1991	Soviet Union breaks into separate states.
1992	Bill Clinton is elected U.S. president.
2000	George W. Bush is elected U.S. president.
2001	Terrorists attack World Trade Towers, New York and the Pentagon, Washington, D.C.

Fast Facts

Official name: Democratic Republic of the Congo

Capital: Kinshasa

Official language: French

Kinshasa

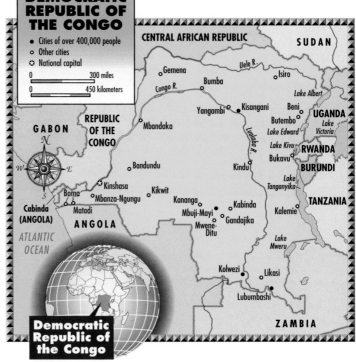

Congo's flag

Congo River

Official religion:	None
Year of founding:	1960
National anthem:	"Arise, Congolese" ("Debout, Congolais")
Government:	Transitional republic, moving toward a representative government
Chief of state:	President
Head of state:	President
Area of country:	905,563 square miles (2,345,410 sq km)
Greatest distance north to south:	Approximately 1,300 miles (2,100 km)
Greatest distance east to west:	Approximately 1,200 miles (1,900 km)
Land and water borders:	It is bordered by the Republic of the Congo, the Central African Republic, Sudan, Uganda, Rwanda, Burundi, Tanzania, Zambia, Angola, and the Atlantic Ocean. The entire length of Lake Tanganyika lies along its eastern border with Burundi and Tanzania. The Congo River forms part of the border with the Republic of the Congo.
Highest elevation:	16,795 feet (5,119 m), at Margherita Peak
Lowest elevation:	Sea level, at the Atlantic Ocean
Highest average temperature:	79°F (26.1°C) in January in Kinshasa
Lowest average temperature:	73°F (22.8°C) in July in Kinshasa
Average annual precipitation:	45 inches (114 cm) in Kinshasa

Hippotamus

Currency

National population: 55,225,478

Population of largest cities:

Kinshasa	6,050,000
Lubumbashi	851,381
Mbuji-Mayi	806,475
Kolwezi	417,810
Kisangani	417,517

Famous landmarks:
- ▶ *Lake Kivu*, Eastern Highlands
- ▶ *Boyoma Falls*, Lualaba River
- ▶ *Margherita Peak*, Ruwenzori Mountains

Industry: Though the majority of Congolese work in agriculture, greater income comes from mining and manufacturing. The major products and their 2000 outputs in metric tons are: crushed stone: 100,000; cement: 96,000; limestone: 25,000; copper: 21,000; cobalt: 4,320; and coltan; 450.

Currency: Congolese franc, which is made up of 100 makuta. As of October 2003, one Congolese franc was worth less than three-tenths of one cent in United States dollars. It would take 422 Congolese francs to equal one U.S. dollar.

System of weights and measures: Metric system

Literacy: 65.5% (2003 est.)

Rural Congolese dress

Dikembe Mutombo

Common words and phrases:

Mbote	Hello
Nakeyi	Goodbye
Sango nini?	How are you?
Limbisa	Please
Matondo	Thank you
Eh	Yes
Te	No

Famous Congolese:

Clementine Faik-Nzuji (1944–)
Author

Joseph Kabila (1972–)
Congo president, following the assassination of his father

Laurent Kabila (1939–2001)
Congo president following overthrow of Mobutu

Simon Kimbangu (1887–1951)
Founder of the Kimbanguist Church

Patrice Lumumba (1925–1961)
First prime minister of the independent Republic of the Congo

Mwadi Mabika (1976–)
WNBA basketball player

Mobutu Sese Seko (1930–1997)
Long-time leader of Congo, then called Zaire

Dikembe Mutombo (1966–)
NBA basketball player

Werrason (Ngiama Noel Makanda) (1965–)
Pop singer

To Find Out More

Nonfiction

▶ Fish, Bruce, Becy Durost-Fish, and Dan Harmon. *Congo: Exploration, Reform, and a Brutal Legacy.* Broomall, PA: Chelsea House Publishers, 2001.

▶ Giles, Bridget, ed. *Peoples of Africa: Peoples of Central Africa.* New York: The Diagram Group, 1997

▶ Heale, Jay. *Democratic Republic of the Congo.* Tarrytown, NY: Marshall Cavendish Corp., 1999.

▶ Kushner, Nina, and Katharine Brown, eds. *Democratic Republic of the Congo.* Milwaukee, WI: Gareth Stevens, 2001.

▶ Mukenge, Tshilemalema. *Culture and Customs of the Congo.* Westport, CT: Greenwood Publishing Group, 2001.

▶ Torres, John Albert. *Sports Great Dikembe Mutombo.* Berkeley Heights, NJ: Enslow Publishers, 2000.

Television Program

▶ *Congo: Heart of Darkness*, a five-part series. ABC News Nightline, anchored by Ted Koppel, 2001.

Web Sites

▶ **Congo Pages**
www.congo-pages.org
An introduction to Congolese life and culture.

▶ **Cultural Profiles Project**
www.settlement.org/cp/english/congo/index.html
Cultural information of Congo.

▶ **The Congo Cookbook**
www.congocookbook.com
Traditional recipes and information about food and cooking.

▶ **African Conservation**
www.africanconservation.com/democraticrepublicofcongo.html
Environmental info and links.

Embassies

▶ **American Embassy Kinshasa**
310 Avenue des Aviateurs
Box 31550
Kinshasa
APO AE 09828

▶ **Canadian Embassy Kinshasa**
P.O. Box 8341
Kinshasa I
Democratic Republic of the Congo

Index

Page numbers in *italics* indicate illustrations.

Meet the Author

TERRI WILLIS believes that beginning research for a new book feels like the start of a journey. "I spend so much time reading and thinking about the countries as I write about them, I sometimes feel as if I'm there," she said.

The journey begins at the local library, where Terri checks out all the materials she can find on a country—books, magazines, videos. She spends days poring over all the information to get a feel for where she'll be going with the book. *King Leopold's Ghost* by Adam Hochschild was a good starting point for this book. Subtitled "A story of greed, terror, and heroism in colonial Africa," the book gave her an understanding of the terror brought on by King Leopold II, and the vast damage he did to the country, in ways that live on today.

Bookstores often provide more materials. Good travel guides can often be very helpful. Then Terri heads to Memorial Library at the University of Wisconsin-Madison. "It's always fun to go back to the campus where I earned my degree," she said. "The library there is full of treasures."

Much of the material from university libraries is very technical and detailed. It takes time to go through the information carefully and present it in a way young people can understand.

The Internet is another good source for material. It's important to use only reliable sources, though, Terri warned. Anybody can create a Web site and put anything on it they want, so not all Internet content is believable. Terri is careful to use only information that comes from such places as universities and government agencies. Even then, she said, it's good to remember that some of these sources may not present the whole picture. A thorough search is important.

Terri fills out her research by talking to people and asking questions. Embassies, chambers of commerce, government agencies, universities—all have knowledgeable people who are willing to help.

Terri has a degree in journalism. Her books include *Libya*, *Romania*, *Vietnam*, and *Venezuela* in the Enchantment of the World series. Other books for Children's Press include *Land Use and Abuse*, *Cars: An Environmental Challenge* (coauthored by Wallace B. Black), and *Restoring Nature, Land*.

Terri lives in Cedarburg, Wisconsin, where she is an educator in the public schools and a Girl Scout leader. She makes her home with her husband, Harry, and their two daughters, Andrea and Elizabeth.

Photo Credits

3 2186 00137 7588